GOING HIGHER:
KEYS TO BECOMING A GENERATION OF LEADERS

By Rickey T. Washington Sr.

RICKEY T. WASHINGTON SR.

Going Higher: Keys to Becoming a Generation of Leaders

Copyright © 2011 by Rickey T. Washington Sr.

All rights reserved.

Published in 2011 by Lyrically Pink Publishing, North Carolina

ISBN: 978-0-9815699-3-2

No part of this publication may be reproduced, stored in a retrieval system, or transmitted in any form or by any means—electronic, mechanical, photocopy, recording, or any other—except for brief quotations in printed reviews, without the prior permission of the publisher. Write to Attention: Permissions, P.O. Box 40864, Baton Rouge, La. 70835

Unless otherwise indicated, all Scripture quotations marked KJV are from the Holy Bible, King James Authorized Version, copyright 1984, International Bible Society. Others are from: The Holy Bible, Amplified Version (AMP), copyright © 1987, The Lockman Foundation; *The Message*. Copyright © 1993, 1994, 1995, 1996, 2000, 2001, 2002. Used by permission of NavPress Publishing Group; New King James Version. (NKJ), copyright © 1982 by Thomas Nelson, Inc. The Living Bible (TLB), copyright © 1996 Tyndale House Publishing. All quotations are used by permission. All rights reserved.

Printed in the U.S.A. First Printed December 2011
Cover design by The Image Garden and Rickey T. Washington Sr.

ACKNOWLEDGMENTS

"Thank you" never seems to be the right words when I think of acknowledging my precious wife of twenty-eight years, Pastor Lesia Washington. Words can never express how grateful to you I am for allowing me the privilege of loving you. To all of those who sowed into my life: Bishop M.B. Jefferson and two people I have served, Pastor Marvin Sapp and my God Father Bishop Rance Allen.

To my Higher Ground Outreach Church Family, thanks for standing with me; to Glennis Gray and Candace Semien who helped pull this vision together; to all my staff who make me look good; and to Lyrically Pink Publishing of North Carolina.

And last but not least, to my children who I love so much, Domonique, Richelle, and Rickey, I dedicate this book to you. One day you will understand.

RICKEY T. WASHINGTON SR.

CONTENTS

Introduction: God Wants You to Get in the Game

Key #1: Become Leadership Material

Key #2: Tap Into Your Leadership Potential.

Key #3: Renew Your Mind

Key #4: Change Your Attitude and Your Altitude

Key #5: Protect the Unity in Your Church

Key #6: Walk in the Fear of the Lord

Key #7: Get Married

Key #8: Bathe in Obedience

Key #9: Release Your Anointing

Key #10: Keep the Fire Burning

Key #11: Decide to Persevere

Key #12: Work with the Team

Key #13: Take the Limits Off

Key #14: Bathe in Courage

Key #15: Stand Loyal

INTRODUCTION

Moses. Jesus. Abraham. Paul. These Biblical leaders were often times challenged—even forced by God—to step out of their comfort zones. Throughout the ages, leaders are tasked with unbelievable challenges. Consider the life of President Abraham Lincoln. Although he was admittedly reluctant about dividing the country over the question of slavery, President Lincoln took a bold stand to end the inhumane practice. Because he faced critics head-on, he thereby established himself as one of America's best presidents. Few would discredit Mahatma Gandhi's accomplishments as a peacemaker. As the pioneer of civil disobedience, Gandhi refused to "fight fire with fire" in order to create harmony during a time when his native India was under extreme political duress.

Many would agree that Dr. Martin Luther King Jr., an admirer of Gandhi's nonviolent tactics, also distinguished himself as one of America's most dynamic leaders. While America faced a turbulent time of instituting civil rights for all, King used the pulpit as his platform to demand justice and equality. He was arrested nearly 100 times, physically assaulted on numerous occasions, and his home was bombed. Still, King walked through the challenges of racism and hatred—leading others to follow in his footsteps and change the countenance of the nation.

Thanks to the rallying efforts of Cesar Chavez, the plight of migrant farm workers in America was brought under the microscope. "Si, si, puede!" *Yes, yes, we can!* Chavez would chant as he went about the country lobbying for higher wages as well as better working and living conditions. In the end, farm workers united and generations of lives were improved because Chavez refused to watch families endure inhumane circumstances.

Let us not forget Oprah Winfrey, the award-winning journalist and entrepreneur whose business ventures tap into the billions!

As daytime TV's most popular talk show host, Winfrey's viewers (or "followers") pick up every book, movie and designer handbag that tops her recommendation list. It's not uncommon to hear people say, "If Oprah says it's good, then it must be good." More importantly, Winfrey uses her television network as a platform to discuss an array of self-help and societal empowerment topics designed to better the world-at-large. As a result, several laws have passed and legislation changed in an effort to improve the lives of women, children and the oppressed.

After being abandoned at birth by his father and put up for adoption by his mother, Steve Jobs dropped out of college and began Apple Computer Inc. Taking on a large vision, Jobs created and developed and redeveloped Apple computers, iPods, iPads, Jobs transformed the way people of all walks used technology. Up to his death in 2011, Jobs released a constant flow of visionary products the world had not imagined before. In fact, the highly anticipated iPhone 4s was released two days after his death, selling out in pre-orders worldwide. Jobs led a team of employees and impacted one billion customers every time they taped the Apple computer screen.

However, not everyone is as charismatic as Gandhi, Chavez, and Winfrey, or as visionary as King and Jobs.

So what's their secret? What does it take to be a leader? Surely even that question baffled Aristotle. As believers we are called to take heed to Jesus' commandment to the apostles: "And he said unto them, Go ye into all the world, and preach the gospel to every creature" (Mark 16:15).

In order to share God's plan with the world, then we, too, must step out of our comfort zones and pick up the responsibility and burden of leadership.

In essence, God wants His children to be leaders. However, sharing God's message of hope and unconditional goodness in a manner that leads people to change lives may be easy for some. Yet, for others, the idea of leading even a small Bible study or prayer group may trigger pools of sweat and quivering stomachs.

Becoming one of God's anointed leaders is an incredible faith walk that transforms your mind, body and soul. This book, *Going Higher: Keys to Becoming a Generation of Leaders*, will teach you how to renew your mind: the conscious, subconscious and conscience. You will discover how dynamic leaders mentally operate, spiritually thrive, and effectively accomplish the tasks God has assigned to them.

Do you jump at the opportunity to lead or do you hide your head in the sand and hope no one notices you? Are you a leader or follower? It's my desire that *Going Higher: Keys to Becoming a Generation of Leaders* will unlock the powerful leader trapped within the crevices of your soul! You are living in a time where your very decisions to lead—or not to lead—can and will affect the next generation. Sure, that's a heavy burden to bear. But, rest assured knowing that the Holy Spirit will help guide you as you press forward in your anointed assignment. Get in the game! The *time* is now for you to step out of your comfort zone. Now is your opportunity to become the leader that God has ordained.

Once you use these principles, it will help in your personal life. It will help you in your marriage, on the job, as a business owner, and as a parent. These keys are principles of life and not just spiritual leadership principles.

The challenges, prayers, and stories in this book will help you to understand your role as a member, youth leader, member of the praise team, intercessor, or minister of helps. Most importantly, when you use the steps in this book, you will push past your limitations and understand that where you are right now is a place of leadership. Because you are an individual with a level of influence on people around you, you **_are_** a leader. And with that comes responsibilities that you now have to take on in order to avoid a curse and to fully move into the promises of God for your life, specifically. I have written this book to believers to successfully employ these strategies for spiritual leadership.

If you don't believe by faith that these things will happen to or for you, then the next chapters of this book are null and void. If you are not in a place of belief, put this book on the shelf and pick up *Called, Appointed, Anointed! Prepare Your Life to be a Vessel for the Anointing and Glory of God* by Janny Grein. It teaches you to walk in the call before someone acknowledges it and appoints you to leadership. Grein will help you walk in the call of leadership on your life so that there is an appointment to leadership. You have to **be** the leader before you are *appointed* to leadership.

When you get to this place of walking in your call and begin your faith walk, your pastor may recognize your anointing and encourage you to assume a leadership role. This book will help guide you *into* that role.

Key #1: Become Leadership Material

The greatest display of leadership is service. Qualified leaders are always in demand. A true leader is authoritative, sacrificial, effective, competent and spiritual. Simply holding a position of importance does not constitute leadership. Taking a consensus or vote does not make you a leader. Resolve does not make you a leader. You could take all the courses you want on how to be a leader and you might still be a follower.

Leadership is born out of character, conflict, and determination. Leadership is the discovery and marriage of purpose, personality and potential. You must assess your personal motivation for leadership. Are you willing to serve? Are you willing to be patient? Are you willing to say, "I'm available?" You may be available, but are you prepared to pay the cost and price of spiritual or Kingdom leadership?

Some people come into leadership with tremendous zeal and little understanding of the dynamics involved. They want to make a difference in this world, but they are not ready for the sacrifices. You are rarely ever prepared to handle leadership responsibilities all at once. Your preparation includes mounting experiences with failures and success. You can only lead others as far as you've gone and are willing to go yourself. Pioneering leaders don't dwell on yesterday's accomplishments and failures. Such innovative people turn disappointments into opportunities to maximize their potential. I believe everyone would *like* to be a leader; that no one wants to be a follower in every situation.

However, many of us do not understand the dynamics of leadership development. Some do not know how to take advantage of opportunities to become leaders. While others do not realize their potential as leaders.

1. Are you willing to make the sacrifice of giving of your time and yourself? This is the biggest thing that leaders don't want to do. You have to sacrifice your feelings your family, where you want be, where you want to go in

order to complete the responsibilities of leadership.
2. Can you find the time to lead aside from the cares of life?
3. Are you answering a call? If you are answering a call and it's an assignment, you will have to do it no matter what. God will put it on the heart to do it. In visions, dreams, and everything you see will tell you that you are suppose to lead and make a difference. Making adjustments in your life.

Your pastor should see the call, the burden on you because you are going to do it. He is going to see it on you, because you will be performing the assignment without the title of leader, you will take on the responsibility of leadership. This is my spot and I have to do it. You will know *this is my assignment!*

Criteria for Leadership

Whoever you are and wherever you are, you can be a spiritual leader. Men and women can be leaders in their homes. Young people can be leaders of their friends. Businessmen, lawyers, doctors and nurses can be leaders in their work place. A leader is simply a person who has a sphere of influence. However, the degree of that influence and the demands it makes on your potential determines the magnitude of your leadership. The janitor is just as important as the CEO. If he, the janitor, doesn't perform his job well, you will have an uncomfortable environment that will affect the performance of the entire organization. Performance management consultant T. Scott Gross teaches his clients that they can "lead from any seat." This is equally true in the Spirit realm.

If you are given any responsibility, no matter how small, you must complete it in excellence. *"And whatsoever ye do, do it heartily as to the Lord, and not unto men" (Colossians* 3:23).

Again, we can look to the Bible for specific examples of characteristics and personality traits that leaders maintain and should maintain especially today: A leader is to be blameless, temperate, orderly, sober minded, steward, and suffer hardship to fulfill the ministry. *(I Timothy 3:2; 2 Timothy 4:5)*

Look at Joseph, who becomes leader in Israel And Joshua, Nehemiah and Rahab. You find leaders of today like President Barak Obama, Desmond Tutu and France's Nicholas Sarkozy who lead with these same character traits. Then there are those who were the opposite and ultimately fell to their own demise.

I agree with Nelson Mandela when he said, "As a leader, there are certain responsibilities which we expect you to observe. One of these is utmost discipline."

Fasting is a critical habit of effective spiritual leaders because it teaches you to deny, control and discipline yourself—by yourself and without any outside, overbearing influence. Fasting is critical to help you remain under the subjection of God and learn self-discipline in passion. Self-denial through fasting helps you to have a keen ear to hear what the Lord says. You have to know God's voice especially as a leader. Fasting makes you deny yourself so you can better hear and obey Him. Fasting is not a requirement to become a leader but it will be something that keeps you leading.

Motivation and Ambition

Regardless of your occupation, the desire to feel like you are the master of your situation and are in control of your environment is a universal emotion. Some have a great longing to be in leadership, while others have only a small desire. However, we each have a leader hidden within. He is crying out to be free. You have selected to read this book because you have the desire to become a dynamic spiritual leader by living out the assignment God's given to you. Even if you're not exactly sure where the desire originated, I'm informing you, having an innate desire is good!

If you are going to be an effective spiritual leader, you must be prepared. You have no option.

As we approach the study of a few basic leadership qualities and characteristics, it is essential that we first cover the foundational principle of the underlying motivation for spiritual leadership. All leadership receives its essence and context from a motivation nuance. The Apostle Paul, one of the greatest leaders in history, expressed it this way: "If anyone sets his heart on being an overseer, he desires a noble task," (I Timothy 3: I). In this verse, Paul clearly states that desiring to be a leader is good. However, some of you may have a hard time accepting that statement because you were raised to believe that leaders should be sought and not the other way around.

Yes, there are ambitions that need to be monitored. Such aspirations are often motivated by greed or lust for power. On the other hand, ambition motivated by a desire to serve is an honorable one. And, a desire to do great is not sinful. What makes it so is the motivation of the heart. Why do you REALLY want to lead? Make sure that God is the ultimate beneficiary.

I believe great leaders are ordinary people who did extraordinary things because circumstances made demands on their potential. History lessons Biblical accounts show leader after leader who become such only after circumstances demanded more from them. Circumstances will pull out of you things that you didn't know where within you.

A circumstance can place on you a demand so great to do something for this generation that surpasses the last. Nehemiah's circumstances pushed him beyond what he could do as a cupbearer. Because no one would take the call, he had to take the call. They say the walls needed to be built up. But because of the call he became a builder and an architect to build back the church walls. He was an ordinary person who did an extraordinary thing strictly because of circumstances that burdened him and demanded more from him. As a leader, God wants to get more from you, and through leadership you will move more to your potential. You get motivated because the cause gets amplified around you and it grows larger, calling for your participation and capacity to responsibly make a difference. That's what makes a great leader.

CHALLENGE

To make sure you are willing to sacrifice look around your life for evidence that you are ready to sacrifice. Are you willing to pay the price and go when you don't feel like it? Can you not be with your spouse and they understand the call? The leadership is the biggest call on your life: to make the sacrifice. I just knew it was something I had to do and I have to do. You will have the burden of leadership. Something will be on you and that will make you lead. It will bother you. That's what Nehemiah had "because of your countenance" it bothers you, you are concerned about it. You can't sleep: I wonder who is taking Bishop to church tonight, does he have the necessities, is she able to prepare the sermon. I had a burden to the small stuff while she handles the big thing. Assistant to make the job easier to spend more time with God and that is the cross that you bear. Are you willing to take the hardship? The call to leadership keeps coming at you. You keep trying not to see but you see it. You try not to dream it, but you do it. It speaks at you. The burden is on you to be concerned about the welfare of the church, of the ministry you are called to, of completing specific task and taking on this responsibility. It speaks. You try not to see it but you see the kids around the church. That's how you know it's your assignment, because it bothers you. It is always coming to you, and you are going to always be tortured by it. It takes over your life. The call is something you will do without the title and without having to be noticed to do. If it's in you to do it, you will do so no matter what. You will proclaim it through hurdles and challenges.

Review your weekly schedule, what time have you set aside for your calling. What time are you willing to sacrifice to do the will God has assigned to you? Create a new schedule that you can commit to—one that includes prayer time and mediation. Push yourself to make honest assessments of how much you will shift and adjust to fulfill this requirement.

Key #2: Tap into Your Leadership Potential

> *He that is faithful in that which is least is faithful also in much: and he that is unjust in the least is unjust also in much. If therefore ye have not been faithful with the unrighteous mammon, who will commit to your trust the true riches? And if you have not been faithful in that which is another man's who shall give you that which is your own? (Luke 16:10-12)*

President Abraham Lincoln was subject to tumultuous periods of depression, yet he was one of America's greatest presidents. Although Moses had speech impairment, he became one of God's most powerful lawgivers. And, Gideon was a coward who rose to be a national hero. Self-confidence is a by-product of our faith in God's faithfulness and ability. True leaders have nothing but themselves to work with. They take the self that God has given them and tap the vast hidden potential that is buried within. Leaders rise to the top in spite of their weaknesses.

By definition, a leader is an innovator. He does things other people either haven't done or won't do. He does things in advance of other people. He makes old things new, and he creates new things. He doesn't set out to do great things or to become a leader, he simply aspires to live life fully and maximize himself. The great leaders of history were people just like you. They were not better, smarter, wiser or more gifted than you; but they developed a passion for life motivated by a deep guiding purpose and a sense of destiny.

Thus, we can say like the Apostle Paul, "I am persuaded that He who has begun a good work in you shall complete it" or "If God be for me, then who can be against me?"

Characteristics of Leadership Potential

There are several characteristics that become more evident in all leaders.

1. Leaders think independently. Every leader should possess the ability to think independently. Good leaders are people who can critically think and reason on their own. Spiritual leaders will not think independently of God and will weigh the opinions and strategies of others before making sound decisions. Could you imagine what would have been the outcome if Moses had asked for the Israelites' recommendations regarding their flight from Egypt? A true leader doesn't follow the crowd. True leaders don't ignore the opinions or contributions of others. They weigh the value of all input and then make their own decisions. An exceptional leader doesn't depend on outside opinions to confirm God's will for his life. If God gives you a command, be very careful when sharing this information to avoid receiving unsolicited negative opinions. Excellent leaders think independently and are brilliant decision makers. Consider Joshua's life. He took the children of Israel into the Promised Land because Moses died before they arrived.

With a bold, authoritative stance, Joshua called the Israelites to make a life-changing choice: *"And if it seem evil unto you to serve the Lord, choose you this day whom ye will serve; whether the gods which your fathers served that were on the other side of the flood, or the gods of the Amorites, including whose land ye dwell: but as for me and my house, we will serve the Lord." (Joshua* 24:15).

Now that's what I call a leader! Notice, he didn't deny that other opinions were available to the Israelites. Joshua didn't deny there were other gods to serve or that the other nations had opportunities that appeared attractive. He simply says, "As for me and my house." Joshua made a decision. Are you an independent thinker?

2. Leaders can act alone when making decisions. Do you perform well independently? Even while using the thoughts of others to the maximum, a leader cannot let others do his thinking or make his decisions. Leaders learn from others, but they are not made by others. Jesus displayed this quality of independent thinking during an encounter with his very own brothers and family. According to John 7: 1-6 (KJV), "*After these things Jesus walked in Galilee: for he would not walk in Judea, because the Jews sought to kill him. Now the Jews feast of tabernacles was at hand. His brethren therefore said unto him, 'Depart hence, and go into Judea, that thy disciples also may see the works that thou doest. For there is not man that doeth anything in secret, and he himself seeketh to be known openly. If thou do these things, show thyself to the world.' For neither did his brethren believe in Him. Then Jesus* *said unto them, My time is not yet come: but your time is always ready."*

Jesus' disciples attempted to influence Him to go to the city and make Himself known to the world. Even in the face of His own family, He declared, "*The right time for me has not come; for you any time is right.*" To be an effective leader, you may listen to all, but in the end, you must be able to act alone because you independently are responsible for your own decisions and how you will lead.

3. Leaders govern themselves. Do you retain control of yourself when facing challenges? The leader who loses self-control in challenging or tempting circumstances forfeits respect and loses influence. He must be calm in crisis and resilient in adversity. True leaders take adversity and turn it into opportunity. Leaders learn by leading and they learn best by directing others in the face of obstacles. As weather shapes mountains, obstacles mold leaders. To be a dynamic leader, you must not only persuade the group to follow you, but you must be able to convince them to trust your judgment abilities despite seemingly insurmountable difficulties. Because you are a Spirit-lead leader, you are going to have to make quality time, quiet time with the Lord for one-on-one direction from the Lord. You cannot govern yourself without that intimate time with God. Remember your assignment is pre-planned. The only way you can walk in it is by spending time with the One who wrote the plan. The only way you can make decisions effectively is by being governed by God.

4. **Leaders can skillfully control anger.** Do you manage your emotions? When someone says something irritating, do you get mad easily? If so, then that is a sign of poor leadership ability. God can't trust you with much because if you are a leader, you're setting yourself up for criticism and a loss of followers. The most visible person is the one who will get all of the criticism. All leaders are targets of criticism. Why? Because leaders are head-and-shoulders above the crowd, elevated, and easily seen. Almost instantaneously, the leader becomes a target. Therefore, you must be able to control yourself and not allow anger to immobilize your rational or moral capacity. Solomon writes, "*Better a patient man than a warrior, a man who controls his temper than one who takes a city,*" (Proverbs 16:32). Solomon advises, *"A wise man is one who controls his temper."* You must maintain control.

5. **Leaders creatively handle disappointments.** Dynamic leaders see disappointments as opportunities to maximize their potential. Such innovative leaders learn from surprises. A standout leader has the ability to stay calm in a crisis. When Jesus and his disciples were out in their boat during a storm, Jesus fell asleep. He was disappointed that they did not have

faith enough to or they didn't know the power they had as leaders to handle the storm. They didn't recognize their own leadership potential and that they had power to calm the storm. I believe that's what happens to every believer: they don't know their leadership potential. Although the disciples possessed this potential, Jesus exemplified his management skills by maintaining control of his disappointment to prevent the apostles from becoming further terrified. Then, he calmed the storm.

Remember the disappointment Moses must have felt when the Israelites reached the Red Sea. Once these, the Israelites started crying out because they were afraid that Pharaoh would catch them. "*And when Pharaoh drew nigh, the children of Israel lifted up their eyes, and, behold, the Egyptians marched after them; and they were sore afraid: and the children of Israel cried unto the LORD,*"(Exodus 14:10). Surely, if even for a split second, Moses was disappointed about reaching the Red Sea while on their way to freedom. Yet, he tapped into that Higher Power. The Israelites could hardly believe Moses when he said to them, "*Fear ye not, standstill, and see the salvation of the LORD,*" (Exodus 14:13). Then Moses ran to God and cried out, "*Lord, Help!*"

Leaders know to maintain self-control during a crisis. That's why they are leaders. Those in charge must skillfully demonstrate coordination capabilities even during somewhat chaotic circumstances. Sometimes, your knees may get shaky, but you must stand. If Moses started crying in front of the people, they also would have cried. This means that your followers will imitate you.

Can you stay calm during a crisis?

Continue asking yourself, "Am I qualified to be a leader?" Leaders maintain peace in adversity, not because they deny its presence, but because they possess self-confidence in purpose, are deeply committed to the vision, and have a complete allegiance in God's divine plan. They are aware of the potential God has placed within them. Excellent leaders are never bound by natural limitations. They see beyond the restrictions and embrace the impossible. How do you handle disappointment? What do you say during a crisis?

A fool uttereth all his mind: but a wise man keepeth it in till afterward. (Proverbs 29:11).

6. Leaders are naturally reliable and show integrity. Can you be entrusted with handling difficult and delicate situations? True leaders are sought out for advice and assistance in delicate circumstances. Daniel is our example of this characteristic. He was a great man of God. When you think of Daniel, do you recall his experience in the lion's den? That was merely a few hours out of Daniel's life. His life is full of leading events orchestrated under God's guiding hand. He served as one of King Darius' three administrators over 120 satraps. (Daniel 6:1).

Daniel was a spirit-filled politician. If you believe that Christians are supposed to be in the background, read the Scriptures again. God wants us where the action is—in the trenches—where Daniel worked on the front lines. Let's look at Daniel's intimate time with God. He knew what God liked and didn't like and Daniel's reaction to God and his relationship with God was so great.

He served with excellence and the king was so impressed that he promoted Daniel to supervise the other administrators. Of course, this made Daniel's co-workers jealous and they began to look for Daniel's imperfections. *"They could find no corruption in him; because he was trustworthy and neither corrupt nor negligent"* (Daniel 6:4). Wouldn't it be wonderful to work with someone who wasn't negligent and unreliable? Trustworthiness is an essential leadership quality.

Daniel's lifestyle included a discipline regiment of prayer and fasting. Yes, fasting and praying, is an ardent leader's responsibility.

CHALLENGE

Set personal time to pray and hear from God. Be sure to establish a regiment of fasting (from food, texting, social networking, etc.) of significance. As a leader you have to take your fasting seriously and passionately. Test your discipline and commitment this week. Get up at 4 a.m. Set this time aside as your intimate time with God where you seek Him for conversation, instructions, and direction. He will tell you whom to talk with, where to go, and people he need you to meet.

Take that time to spend with God. We've gotten fasting down and not the other component of replacing the fasted item with time with God. When you fast without replacement, all you're doing is torturing yourself.

Review your sacrifice schedule from Key #1's challenge and stretch your fasting and prayer time. Keep record of what God tells and shows you.

Key #3: Renew Your Mind

Throughout school and work, we have learned that what stands between you and your desired success is your decision-making strategy and ability. In order to improve the quality of your leadership capacity, you must change your way of thinking. The Bible strongly exhorts the believer to work at renewing their mind. You and I are responsible for the development of and the management of our thought life. The Scripture strongly supports this, saying:

> *That ye put off concerning the former conversation with the old man, which is corrupt according to*

the deceitful lusts; And be renewed in the spirit of your mind. (Ephesians 4:22-23).

The success of a leader begins with them leading their own mind and their thought life: *Beloved, I wish above all things that thou mayest prosper and be in health, even as thy soul (mind, will, and emotion) prospereth* (3 John 2).

Soul is another term for mind. There are several Scripture references regarding a rejuvenation of the thought process. *"And be renewed in the spirit of your mind."* (Ephesians 4:23). *"And be not conformed to this world: but be ye transformed by the renewing of your mind, that ye may prove what is that good, acceptable, and perfect will of God."* (Romans 12:2).

When the Bible speaks of renewing the mind, it is talking about the transformation of your decision-making process. The thought patterns you choose to adopt for your life will dramatically affect the quality of your evaluation method. We bring our old inferior thought patterns into the Kingdom of God when we are born again. But, the new birth does not instantly change our behavior or thought process. We are ever evolving through the process of renewing the mind and conscientious discipline. "*Casting down imaginations, and every high thing that exalteth itself against the knowledge of God, and bringing into captivity every thought to the obedience of Christ; And having in a readiness to revenge all disobedience, when your obedience is fulfilled"* (2 Corinthians 10:4-5).

To understand this route, you must first comprehend the unique way that God created us as humans. The Bible explains that we have been created as *tripartite* (three) creatures. We are spirit beings who live inside physical bodies, and possess a soul. The soul of man has five basic components: the *mind, will, imagination, emotions* and *intellect*. The soul determines a person's unique personalities and characteristics. The spirit is eternal and will continue to exist long after the physical death of a human. God chooses to work within the framework of how He has created us to accomplish His will in our lives. *"And the very God of peace sanctify you wholly: and I pray your whole body, soul and spirit be preserved blameless unto the coming of our Lord Jesus Christ"* (I Thessalonians 5:23).

God does not wave a magic wand over our heads to cause an immediate transformation of our thought life, but instead operates within systematic procedures that He has designed to change or establish our thinking.

Those procedures are disciplined prayer, fasting, and meditation on His word. We can look at Joshua 1 again to understand this. The death of Moses changed Joshua life. He was the assistant to Moses, and now he is appointed the leader. Suddenly, he is no longer the servant; he is the leader. In telling Joshua to become the new leader, God says, I know you are scared but I am going to be with you. And then we begin to see in Joshua 1:8, the process for getting Joshua to move from a follower's mind to a leader's mind. God tells him in essence that you are not going to be a servant anymore, you are going to be a leader; here is what you are going to need to do it: "mediate on the Word". He is dealing with Joshua's mind and his thinking. For God to keep telling him to be courageous means he was afraid. He was under the other mindset of being a servant and it would be through the meditation that he would become a successful leader.

The Bible teaches that the spirit and soul are closely interwoven and can only be divided and understood in light of the Word of God. Our soul or mind can only be transformed in line with how God created our minds to function and that includes constant meditation.

There are three components of the mental complex: conscious mind, subconscious mind, and conscience mind. These three components operate together in a dynamic systemic way as the mental computer that keeps our lives on course.

The conscious mind handles the purposeful conscious thoughts and day-to-day decisions. It controls the initial reasoning and logical thinking that requires concentration.

The subconscious component is the autopilot of the mind. It is responsible for carrying out the decisions of the conscious component. Once the conscious mind has processed a situation and accepted certain norms and values as truth, the subconscious mind takes over. The reason being, a choice has been made and little conscious thought is required.

Our subconscious can access our belief and value systems and make decisions at a "sub" or below conscious level at all times. This is a valuable asset. Think about it. When I drive up to a stoplight, I do not have to purposefully concentrate and rethink my next actions. The process is pretty much automatic, thanks to the assistance of the subconscious. After a procedure is repeatedly acted out, the subconscious is prepared to take control the next time the same or a similar situation occurs.

And the third component, the conscience mind, is the storehouse for our belief and value systems. This is the reference point where all circumstances are judged. This part of the mental complex is the heart of the thought process. Here is where all things are determined based upon preconceived standards. As situations occur in life, this standard of judgment develops and evolves as the processing center of truth.

The subconscious accesses information in the conscience and reaches decisions on an ongoing basis without much thought. When the conscious mind processes information, the rationale and value systems are stored in the conscience, where it can later be accessed by the conscious to make purposeful determinations.

Unfortunately, renewing the mind has long been misunderstood as meaning that a believer should excel in Scripture knowledge and memorization. This could not be farther from the truth. To have a renewed mind is to function in accordance with a new value and belief system—one synchronized with the Word of God and presence of the Holy Spirit. Far too often, you'll see many believers think they have transformed their mind because they know the Scriptures and can quote chapters and verses. And they think that is "it" as far as renewing one's mind. Sadly, they have no knowledge of what pleases God. The Bible refers to such individuals as carnal Christians and babes in Christ.

There is a reason why so many good Christians wrestle in an internal war of wanting to do the right thing and yet seem to be locked into unrighteous behavior. As the conscience stores the values and beliefs that govern our lives, it is stacking information on top of information. The more we learn, the more we store. Think of it as two sections in this conscience compartment: the before-the-knowledge-of-Christ (BC) section and the after-the-knowledge–of-Christ (AC) section.

For years, the subconscious has always accessed information from the BC value department, and this old information is what was believed to be the most reliable—a type of preconceived truth. Even when a man is reborn, the subconscious still accesses information from the BC department first. It requires a great deal of purposeful effort for the subconscious to switch gears and access information from the AC section. Why? Because the subconscious does not yet see this information as being reliable. Normally, after many struggles, mistakes, failures, sweat and tears coupled with meditating and intimate time with God, the subconscious is finally retrained to access data from the AC section. Eventually, it becomes easier to make righteous decisions.

In essence, to renew the mind means to transform the mental complex operation within yourself so that all choices are based on Biblical truth and not on experiential information that has been gathered over a lifetime and may or may not be accurate.

The transformation process is challenging simply because of how God designed us to function. We don't change easily. Having a strong will is good. Otherwise, it would be difficult to maintain any kind of stable character or behavior with a man who has an easily manipulated judgment standard. Ephesians 4:22-23 stress the need to examine the spirit of your mind: *"Strip yourselves of your former nature [put off and discard your old unrenewed self] which characterized your previous manner of life and becomes corrupt through lusts and desires that spring from delusion. And be constantly renewed in the spirit of your mind [having a fresh mental and spiritual attitude], And put on the new nature (the regenerate self) created in God's image, [Godlike] in true righteousness and holiness."* (AMP)

We are uniquely designed and constructed by God with an on-board steering system: The heart of the system is self-image. Our self-image is the predetermined belief of what we think we can become, how we respond to others, and how others will respond to us. The definitions and expectations of our self-image and self-worth are part of the information stored in the conscience (belief) system. This stored information sets the coordinates of the internal guidance system.

You have probably heard the old adage: "Let your conscience be your guide." That train of thought is normally accepted as a positive statement if the conscience has been properly trained and developed. But what happens if the conscience has not been properly trained or is underdeveloped? As a potential leader it is especially critical for you to take extra effort to develop God-defined self-image and God-guided conscience.

"Howbeit when he, the spirit of truth, is come, he will guide you into all truth; for he shall not speak of himself: but whatsoever he shall hear, that shall he speak: and he will show you things to come" (Exodus 20:5; John 16:13KJV).

Coming into truth happens when the Holy Spirit communicates with your *human spirit*, who in turn gives relevant information to your *conscious mind*. You have probably called your fact an inspired thought or idea. Many times, you have said that "something" told you about a truth or situation. You most likely heard the voice of your human spirit which heard directly from the Holy Spirit!

As a leader, you must develop that "hearing," make decisions, and take action based on what you heard from the Lord.

The Evolution of the Conscience

The conscience is the belief or value system that you have developed over time. Its evolution has been influenced by four key elements that work to shape our values and beliefs into decision-making criteria, including: social environment, credible authority figures, repetitious information, and personal experiences.

Our social environment helps shape what we believe about the world around us. In our developing years, we were totally naïve in our thinking, but as we began to mentally develop, the social environment begins to impose certain perceived truths about life. Such information continually influences the shaping of our value system. Secondly, people of authority like our parents, older relatives, teachers and ministers continue molding our conscience and value system. Those we are told to respect and obey greatly influence how and what we choose to believe about life.

Thirdly, our minds are designed to accept information that is input on a consistent and repetitious basis. Whatever you repeatedly hear eventually makes its way into your thought process and helps to shape your values, judgments, and leadership potential. This is the basis for how the multi-billion dollar advertising industry continues to flood consumers with their "must have" products. It has been proven that **when** you see or hear something repetitiously, then the object will tend to alter your thought process, and possibly, your belief system. A personal experience makes the most potent impact on what we believe about any situation.

Your belief system would be most influenced by your personal experience rather than by what you hear from me, the manufacturer of a product, or recent statistics. Experiencing something firsthand even supersedes what you may have witnessed when watching someone else react to the same circumstances. And, a personal experience is never at the mercy of the most profound arguments. In essence, what you go through makes the most significant impact on your belief system.

Think about it. Once you have completed a task, the mind compiles and processes that information for future retrieval. This frees most of the conscious mind up for involvement in other areas, while the autopilot (subconscious) handles the previously learned task. Our subconscious seems to protect the beliefs that we have consciously accepted and established by keeping us (through our decisions) automatically in line with it. This is the greatest asset to the development of Godly character and faithfulness. Without the benefit of the subconscious, we would have to re-think every accepted moral value each time we are faced with a decision.

The subconscious mind has the task of accessing and handling reality as it is perceived by the will of the conscious mind, and keeping the individual locked into a belief system.

The question then arises, *if my subconscious mind is doing all this work, what role does the Holy Spirit have?* The existence of your brain, heart or other organs does not diminish or nullify the role of the Holy Spirit in your life. The Bible speaks of the Holy Spirit's role in the life of the believer: to "assist him in living the God-kind of life." In the same manner that the spirit of God works with the believer's physical organs (his mouth and his body) God uses the Holy Spirit to help coordinate the mental faculties of man. Remember now, the subconscious does not function solely nor independently of the conscious mind. It simply serves the conscious mind in the long-term operation of the belief system. It is the conscious mind of the leader that depends on Holy Spirit to communicate with it—to bear witness—to give guidance and direction for living and for leading others. More importantly, the conscious mind of the spiritual leader relies upon the Holy Spirit to help it determine what is and isn't true. *"The spirit itself (Himself) beareth witness with our spirit, that we are the children of God"* (Romans 8:16KJV). In 1 Corinthians 2:10, the Scripture further explains, *"But God hath revealed them unto us by his spirit: for the spirit searcheth all things, yea the deep things of God."*

Once the conscious mind has received information it deems to be reliable (in this case, spiritual truth) and establishes it as truth, the conscious mind allows the "right of passage" of that truth into the conscience to be accepted by the subconscious mind.

There, the subconscious mind automatically directs the leader in line with the wishes of the Holy Spirit. You don't need to fear the subconscious mind because it only serves you based on how it has been instructed to perform.

Although the function of the subconscious mind is intended to be good as it works to carry out the wishes of the conscious, it may not be serving your best interest. If somewhere along life's way, you accepted something that was a false truth—because you thought it was true at the time—that acceptance caused your belief system to be misinformed.

If your subconscious mind has locked in false information that it believes to be true, then your subconscious mind will operate on that information. Thus, your life will be directed in agreement with something that is wrong or not true. And, while you consciously know the truth, your subconscious mind will not automatically release that "old truth" (which is really a lie that you thought was true) and replace it with the correct truth. What's more, the autopilot is strong and too consistent to be so easily changed. It, therefore, continues to operate and direct your life by the old truth until properly instructed to *release* (or erase) the old and lock onto the new information. Remember, the language of the conscious and subconscious mind: It has the three-dimensional linguistics of words, images and feelings. Once the new information is accepted, this dynamic system gives birth to thoughts which transform into images, feelings and non-auditory communication on the silver screens of our imagination.

We build our belief systems through what we think, experience and receive through meditation. Essentially, thoughts become the three-dimensional language of the conscious and subconscious mind through Biblical study and meditation.

Although an incident may occur only once, the more you reflect on it, the more it happens to you (i.e. instant replay) in the arena of your imagination. That pivotal experience has a dynamic impact on your life. Eventually, over a period of time, the thoughts vividly imagined assimilate into your belief system replacing the old information.

For instance, have you ever remembered an event and noticed that just as your memories intensified you felt similar, if not the same, feelings as when the incident occurred? There is no doubt why we are encouraged in the Scriptures to meditate on the Word of God continuously. According to Psalms 1:2, we are told to meditate in the word of God day and night. God knows how we function and instructs us on how to change internally which eventually causes the outward transformation (1 Timothy 4:15-16KJV). The Scriptures have a plethora of occasions where the concept of repetitious thinking and recall are commanded. This is success mediation, the language of the subconscious and conscience at its best. God instructs you to communicate with your internal programming mechanisms to change you and, in the end, your situation. Emotional information that is presented for you on a continuous basis will ultimately gain mental consent (right of passage) and become part of your belief system. Consider what Paul wrote to the people at Corinth:

> *Casting down imaginations, and every high thing that exalteth itself against the knowledge of God, and bringing into captivity every thought to the obedience of Christ" (2 Corinthians 10:5).*

You will have to get rid of thoughts and imaginations that are keeping you away from leading. The negative talk and negative thinking that your teacher, brother, mother, etc., have all have to be casted down in order to lead. My fifth grade teacher said I would never speak publically and I had to cast that down. Where would I be if her words had stopped me? You have to cast down all the negative experiences, thoughts, and instant replays that say you can't be what God calls you to be. Jeremiah said no one in his family had ever done this, and even with those thoughts God decidedly proclaimed Jeremiah would change a generation and do something he had never done before. Jeremiah had to cast down the thought that this could never be done. As a leader, you too have to daily grasp and discard thoughts and imaginations that come: i.e. thoughts that say, "you won't build a great church", "you won't have an impact", "or "someone else can do it better than you". You have to cast it down or you will always only be a follower when God has called and chose you to lead.

Remember, it is through meditation on God's word that the mind renews. The word meditation by definition means to mutter, practice beforehand and envision. There are three components of Biblical meditation: verbalization, visualization and internalization. Such elements encompass and address the basic components of an experience. Remember, an experience is composed of words, emotions and images. Verbalization is the foundational factor of meditation; and for leaders, it is the most essential. The desire of our heart is upon that which we meditate, and must be based on the Word of God. As we begin to speak God's words, two key actions take place.

First, words create image so when we verbalize what God's word says about our circumstances, we are able to get a mental picture of God's will for our lives. Secondly, when we speak faith-filled words, it is that action that releases faith into the situation and triggers divine assistance.

An effective leader takes all situations and plans to God, to meditate on, to internalize, to visualize, and to internalize the solutions that only come from time with God.

CHALLENGE

Start tonight at bedtime. Take time to record every negative word, every bad thought, and every hurtful circumstance of the day. Pray against it. Pray that every negative thing not be rooted in your heart but instead fall off of you immediately. As you pray, scratch them off the list with a black permanent marker. Follow this up with a statement of strength and plan time in the next day to repeatedly announce the statement of strength and keep positive thoughts ahead of you as a new foundation for your mind's renewal.

Key #4: Change your Attitude and your Altitude

When Paul wrote the epistle to the Romans, he created a "guidebook" for the Gentiles (new believers) on how to follow the righteousness of God during their faith walk. Paul repeatedly encouraged the Romans to remain steadfast in faith as they learned how to prevent falling back into iniquity. In the Amplified Bible, Romans 8:8 states, *"So then those who are living the life of the flesh/catering to the appetites and impulses of their carnal nature/cannot please or satisfy God, or be acceptable to Him."* The Amplified Bible tells us that to live by the flesh is to cater to the appetites and impulses of the carnal or fleshly nature. In essence, your lifestyle and impulses will determine your success in leadership.

We have all been to banquets and other events that were catered. It's always fun to be waited on and to have our wants and needs fully met—immediately—by someone else. But, there is a relentless price to be paid for that kind of service. The same is true when you consider your attitude. You must pay for falling into the position of catering to the desires and demands of self which is our attitude and emotions or what the Bible calls "flesh" in Romans 8:6.

In Biblical terms, flesh is the system of sense and reason without the Holy Spirit. For many, flesh ultimately leads to death—both physically and spiritually. Death comprises all the miseries arising from sin, both here and in the hereafter. But, the mind of the Holy Spirit is life and peace (spiritually) both now and forever. This means that if you and I follow the dictates and demands of our attitude and our unbridled emotions, we will have a hefty price to pay.

The Apostle Paul explains in Romans 8:7, the mind of the flesh with its carnal thoughts and purposes is hostile to God, for it does not submit itself to God's law, indeed it cannot. Part of the price we must pay for gratifying our fleshly desires is not being able to live the Spirit-filled life. *"For those who are living according to the flesh and are controlled by its unholy desires set their minds on and pursue those things that gratify the flesh, but those who are according to the Spirit and are controlled by the desires of the Spirit set their minds on and seek those things which gratify the [Holy] Spirit."* (Romans 8:5).

The Bible clearly teaches that the flesh is opposed to the Spirit, and the Spirit is opposed to the flesh. They are continually antagonistic toward each other. This means that we cannot be led by our attitude and still be led by the Holy Spirit. We have to make a choice. That single decision will determine your stress factor. It will also establish your ability to turn hate into love; rejection into accomplishment; and transform fear into triumph. That particular option is also how you choose to react to what has been done to you in the past or is happening to you right now. Essentially, your attitude will determine your success in life.

Let me give you my definition of an attitude in a series of four statements:

1. Your attitude is an inward feeling expressed by outwardly behavior.
2. Your attitude is seen by all without you saying a word.
3. Your attitude is the advance man of your true self.

4. The roots of your attitude are hidden, but its fruit is always visible.

Your attitude is your best friend and your worst enemy. Your manner either draws people toward you or repels people. Your stance determines the quality of your relationships with your spouse, children, employer, friends and God Almighty.

Unfortunately, some of us choose to have bad attitudes, and others are all too vocal about such negative attitudes. However, your attitude does not have to be a permanent stance. Decide to change your attitude right now. After all, your attitude is a choice. You choose your attitude every morning when you wake up. King David writes in Psalm 118:24 (NKJV), *"This is the day that the Lord has made we will rejoice and be glad in it."* If you woke this morning and did not find your picture in the obituary column, get happy, rejoice, and be glad.

Choose to have a good attitude as soon as you rise in the morning. What kind of attitude did you choose this morning? Was it, "Good morning, Lord" or "Good Lord, is it morning?" A positive attitude is a choice that some people make, despite their problems. The past is the past—not the present.

Your attitude will help a very stern person be received properly. A strong leader can give direction and take their ministry a lot further. Your attitude is your best friend or your worst enemy.

With the wrong attitude no one will follow you. You have to decide to change your attitude for people to see your love and concern. You cannot be a spiritual leader without loving people.

The best way to guarantee your success in life is to forget the past. The Apostle Paul offered some of the greatest advice a mortal can accept when he writes, "*Forgetting those things which are behind,*" (Philippians 3:13, NKJV). Don't become stifled by yesterday's accomplishments or yesterday's failures. You must remember, it is impossible to succeed without experiencing failure. A man who never failed is a man who never accomplished anything. The greatest waste of energy in America is not electricity or natural gas. We waste emotional and intellectual energy fighting the inevitable situations of life. We must clearly understand: You cannot change certain things in life such as the death of a loved one.

Hebrews 9:27 (KJV) declares, "*For as it is appointed for men to die once.*" When you fight the inevitable circumstances in life, you often grow bitter and resentful. You become twisted, negative and hateful. Some actually die because of their inability to move beyond these painful, inevitable situations. Get this thought into your mind and repeat it until it is etched into your brain. THE PAST IS OVER! I want to teach you one of the most therapeutic phrases in human speech. Everyone goes through adversity, rejection and reversal. The phrase to remember in times like these is this: Get over it!

Have you been betrayed? Get over it! Have you failed? Get over it!

It would be impossible to estimate the number of lost jobs, missed promotions, ruined marriages and churches that have been destroyed by whiny, thumb-sucking, pity pat people without grit, focus or fortitude. The Apostle Paul writes in 1 Thessalonians 5:18 (NKJV), *"In everything give thanks."* Now, consider the converse and give thanks. In heartache, give thanks. In pain, poverty or prosperity, give thanks. "*Be thankful to Him, and bless His name. For the Lord is good; His mercy is everlasting.*" (Psalm 100:4-5, NKJV). God is greater than the criticism you are facing. He is bigger than the giants you are facing. He is higher than the mountains you are climbing. He is more powerful than the burdens you are carrying. You cannot take the worst of your past into your future leadership role.

CHALLENGE

True leadership is knowing your attitudes, your strengths, and your weaknesses without staying in your past or allowing the bad to move into your future. Began to place the right people around you who can help you turn into who you need to become.

I challenge you to chart your attitudes, strengths, and weakness under four columns labeled "good," "bad," "keep", and "forget". Now, take mental, internal, personal, and intimate inventory of what you are doing. What are your good attitudes? What are the bad attitudes? (Let me note, if the attitude isn't "good" then it is "bad". Don't allow yourself to have a gray area in this evaluation). What attitudes should you keep and what attitudes do you need to drop like a hot potato? List them, honestly and with conviction to keep or drop and forget them. Continue these steps with your strengths and weaknesses. You will find at the end that you have created a self-approved list of character traits that you can now magnify daily as you walk in your call of leadership.

Key #5: Protect the Unity in Your Church

It is our job as leaders to safeguard the harmony of our church. Unity in the church is so important that the New Testament places more emphasis on this concept than exploring Heaven or Hell. In Ephesians 4:3 (NCV) the Apostle Paul writes, "You are joined together with peace through the spirit, so make every effort to continue together in this way." God deeply desires that we experience oneness and harmony with one another. In another letter, the Apostle Paul emphasizes in Colossians 3:14 (TLB), "Most of all, let love guide your life, for then the whole church will stay together in perfect harmony."

Unity is the soul of fellowship. Destroy it and you rip the heart out of Christ's body. Unity is the66 essence, the core, of how God intends for us to experience life together in His church. Our supreme model for unity is the Trinity. The Father, Son and Holy Spirit are completely unified as one. God Himself is the highest example of sacrificial love, humility and perfection. Just like every parent, our Heavenly Father enjoys watching His children get along peacefully. In his final moments before his arrest, Jesus prayed passionately for our unity. Interestingly, it was our unity that was of upmost importance in Christ's mind during those agonizing hours. This fact demonstrates the significance of this subject. Nothing on Earth is more valuable to God than His church. He paid the highest price for it, and He wants it protected, especially from the devastating damage that is caused by division, conflict and disharmony. It is your responsibility as a spiritual leader to safeguard the unity where you fellowship. In fact, you are commissioned by Jesus Christ to do everything possible to preserve the unity, shield the fellowship, and promote harmony in your church family and among all believers.

The fourth Keys of Ephesians continuously declares, "Make every effort to keep the unity of the Spirit throughout the bond of peace."

Unity means to cause something to adhere, bond or stick to another; in one accord or one spirit. The Apostle Paul pleads to the people regarding this issue in I Corinthians 1:10 (NKJV):

Now, dear brothers and sisters, I appeal to you by the authority of the Lord Jesus Christ to stop arguing among yourselves. Leaders lead with class and harmony. Let there be real harmony so there won't be divisions in the church. I plead with you to be of one mind, united in thought and purpose.

By writing, "brothers and sisters," Paul is emphasizing that all Christians are part of God's diverse family. Believers share a unity that flows even deeper than that of blood brothers and sisters. To "let there be real harmony," allow for no "divisions," and "be of one mind united in thought and purpose," does not require anyone to believe exactly the same. There is a difference between having opposing viewpoints and being divisive. A group of people will not completely agree on every issue, but they can work together harmoniously if they agree on what truly matters: Jesus Christ is Lord of all. In your church, you should speak and behave in a manner that will reduce arguments and increase harmony. Petty differences should never divide Christians.

Saddleback Church pastor Rick Warren offers these steps to ensure unity within the church family:

1. Focus on what we have in common, not our differences.

2. Be realistic in your expectations of others.
3. Choose to encourage one another rather than criticize.
4. Refuse to listen to gossip!
5. Practice God's method for conflict resolution.

To that I will add, **support your pastor.** There are no perfect leaders, but God gives spiritual leaders the responsibility and the authority to maintain unity in the church. During interpersonal conflicts, the role of the leader is a thankless job. Pastors and leaders often have the unpleasant task of serving as a mediator between hurt, conflicting or immature members. Leaders are also given the impossible task of trying to make everyone happy, which even Jesus could never accomplish!

You should still be responsive to your pastoral leaders. Listen to their counsel. Ministers are alert to the condition of your lives and work under the strict supervision of God. Even as a leader yourself, you should contribute to the joy of their leadership; don't drudge it. Make it a point to offer your assistance at all times. Church ministers and spiritual leaders will one day stand before God and give an account of how well they watch over their followers. But, you are accountable, too. You will give an account to God of how well you followed your leaders.

As leaders, you will be accountable for other members who the pastor has placed under your supervision. That is the law of delegated authority. God gave the authority to your leader, then the leader gave the authority to you. Always remember you are working the vision given to you.

In the tenth chapter of Numbers, God puts the leader's (Moses') spirit on the elders. That is why, in order to keep unity in church, all spiritual leaders should stay in line with how well we as leaders follow our leader in order to keep the unity in the church. You will walk in the authority of your leader and possess what is called "delegated authority". You are walking under the power of your leader, your pastor. You will operate under the authority that has been given to you. The authority on you is as of the leader. So you support the pastor and protect the unity of the church because you are under the anointing of the pastor.

CHALLENGE

Remember to treat the Pastor's larger vision like it's your own even though it originated with someone else. Spend a moment in prayer and honest thoughts now evaluating yourself. Remind yourself that you are carrying another man's vision. Write the question, "What would Bishop do?" in your heart and let it reside in your mind. As you handle situations, this question helps you make sure that you are handling the vision correctly. How would Bishop handle the problem? How would Bishop do this? Did I handle this task within the larger vision? Did I have myself in this? Was it more of God or more of me? Was I under delegated authority and following pastoral leadership or my own? When you handle a task, you were talking on Bishop's behalf. You will do a lot of things that your name will not be spoken. Can you handle this? If not, how do you plan to clear your mind to be do this?

Maintain your reverence and respect for your leader and operate in the fear of the Lord to work toward the vision. When you consider your level of reverence for your leader, can you operate selfishly and respectfully? If you find that your leader is a person you cannot respect and reverence, you should not be under their leadership, because you will not prosper.

Key #6: Walk in the Fear of the Lord

As Christians, we are often called upon to "walk by faith and not by sight," where we are moved to serve based upon our fear of the Lord. *"By faith, Noah, being warned of God of things not seen as yet, moved with fear, prepared an ark to the saving of his house; by the which he condemned the world, and became heir of the righteousness which is by faith"* (Hebrews 11:7). Although Noah's generation had never seen rain, his fear of the Lord empowered him to withstand being mocked and ridiculed by his peers. Noah worked diligently for 120 years to create a monumental ship that would sustain many lives.

What does the term God-fearing mean? The expression is defined as reverence; recognizing God as omnipotent, omnipresent and omnificent: He is the great "I am." As leaders, we must walk in the fear of the Lord. The Bible says only a fool says in his heart "there is no God". Fear is the key that unlocks miracles in the supernatural (Acts 2:41-43, 5: 10-12). In the book of Acts, there are numerous incidents where divine judgment always preceded great moves of God. With an absolute fear of God, you would forgive a person who injured you greatly.

Observe this pattern. Not only did the early church have great power, but they had great joy, miracles, outpouring of the Holy Ghost and gifts of the spirit. The book of Acts also documents numerous incidents where believers experienced discernment, signs and wonders, shouts of praise, and all-night prayer meetings. During this time, about 85 A.D., all of the new believers were walking in the fear of the Lord. Eventually, we will all feel a deeper fear of the Lord before His return.

Please don't play with God. Meaning, God does not need a lukewarm disciple: either you have the faith of a mustard seed or you have no faith. Don't try to wade in between the two extremes. Of course, He is a God of grace, but you can fall from grace.

Unfortunately, many leaders have fallen back into iniquity. God is also long-suffering. When God's leaders are living loose, the church body can get away with everything. *"Wherefore I say unto you, All manner of sin and blasphemy shall be forgiven unto men: but the blasphemy against the Holy Ghost shall not be forgiven unto men,"* (Matthew 12:31).

As you well know, God uses yielded vessels (men and women)—not golden or perfect vessels. Remember, Peter cursed and denied the Lord thrice, yet he was forgiven. King David also sinned a number of times, including when he called a census of the children of Israel. This angered the Lord who caused a pestilence to destroy 70,000 men because numbering a population was strictly forbidden in Hebraic law (2 Samuel 24: 117). Yet, King David still reigned and was known as the leader who "had God's heart." Why? Because David still served with an unashamed fear of the Lord. *"But as for me, I will come into thy house, in the multitude of thy mercy: and in thy fear will I worship toward thy holy temple"* (Psalm 5:7, *KJV*).

Prior to reaching the city of Gerar, Abraham had been walking in fear of God. However, Abraham knew that this was an ungodly environment and he was overtaken by his own fear of being killed by King Abimelech who desired Sarah, Abraham's wife. Thus, Abraham disobeyed God by giving his wife, Sarah, to King Abimelech. *"But God came to Abimelech in a dream by night, and said to him, Behold, thou are but a dead man, for the woman which thou hast taken; for she is a man's wife"*

(Genesis 20:3). As you can see, God revealed Himself to Abimelech, who then came to fear the Lord and returned Sarah to Abraham.

The most dangerous person is one who has no fear of God (2 Peter 2: 10-12, Romans 1: 18, Proverbs 1:24-29). God will let you party, leave you alone and wait for you to repent (Daniel 5:1-5). However, when you cross the line and tempt God by talking of spiritual matters without proper knowledge, you will face consequences. In fact, many spiritual leaders believe that they can get away with anything because they are the pastoral shepherds of designated flocks. Not so. Remember, judgment on you will be greater because you were appointed by God to lead.

Let's examine Belshazzar. He got weighed in the balance with God and was found wanting and later slain (Daniel 5:27). King Nebuchadnezzar ate grass until he admitted that God is God (Daniel 5:21). It is the fear of God that brings on the move of the Holy Spirit. Because when you reverence God—who He is—then He manifests Himself. King David said, "I will worship God in the fear of the Lord." You praise God for His acts, works, testimonies, deeds and miracles. But, you should worship God for who He is! You should bow your knees willingly on a daily basis because every knee will bow and every tongue will confess.

Saul found out that who one fears is the same that one obeys. Prophets told him God said to not spare man or beast, and that what Saul hid in tents or secrets whispered must be killed. However, Saul admitted that he feared and obeyed people!

God-fearing people obey God.

The bottom line is you have to fear God in order to obey Him. When you don't fear God and He tells you to do something, you probably will not obey.

As Christians, we should fear God too much not to obey Him. I have disobeyed God before and it's not fun! He chastens with the painful rod of correction. Obedience is far better than sacrifice. God doesn't give you cancer, rip your legs off or poke your eyes out. But, He knows how to get your attention. "The fear of the Lord will add days to your life, but the years of the wicked shall be shortened," (Proverbs 10:27, NKJV). The devil wants your worship, and he receives it whenever you don't fear God. Thus, brokenness and death is the price you pay for not fearing God.

"Moreover thou shalt provide out of all the people, able men, such as fear God, men of truth, hating covetousness; and place such over them, to be rulers of thousands, and rulers of hundreds, rulers of fifties and rulers of tens." (Exodus 18:21).

As with the men of Exodus, you are able to lead because you fear God. You give God honor and therefore He will honor you will all His substance. Pastors and spiritual leaders have authority over you because you fear God. Think about it. You submit to all of your leaders and allow them to speak to you in a way that you wouldn't allow anyone else because you fear God. That is the definition of submission.

You are to first submit yourself to God then to your pastor by the will of God (2 Corinthians 8:5). Without the fear of God, we wouldn't submit to anybody. We are children of wrath and rebellion by nature, the Bible says. As a leader appointed by God, your assignment is to be loyal, faithful, a supportive armor bearer and understanding of your pastor's shortcomings. Sure, there will be countless incidents where your pastor will seem short or have a difficult attitude. But, you are to stay true blue.

If God-fearing men and women do not honor their leader, then those members must deal directly with God. He says that when you appoint a man in church, you are to make sure that he is God-fearing. If not, the lawless member will be a thorn in your flesh and a plank in your eye (Deuteronomy 4:9-10). Not only am I to fear God, but I'm to teach my children to fear the Lord. Unfortunately, some children don't fear God because they didn't receive training during childhood. It's only obvious when you give some children everything they want, and wonder why they turn out bad. You have to train children. If you don't have kids in church, then not only will they suffer, but you as parents will have to answer to God.

Let's take a look at Nehemiah. He chose Hanani as a ruler of the palace because Hanani was a faithful man (Nehemiah 7:2). Hanani was not only faithful, but he was also trustworthy, a confidante, constant, devoted and true. Above all, Hanani feared God. The people that God exalts are faithful and God-fearing. God does not exalt you for latency, but because you are faithful and fear Him. As an effective leader, you must follow the mandate of Ecclesiastes 9:13 *(KJV)* which admonishes us to, "Fear God, and keep his commandments: for this is the whole duty of man."

CHALLENGE

God fearing deals with encompassing a different aspect of your relationship with God which includes you knowing Him, understanding Him fully and doing so through time and study of His word. It requires you to honor God as God.

Have you really given your heart to God? Is He Lord of every aspect of your life? Write down when you have not placed your total trust in God for your life? Where have you not committed your life to Him? List them and repent of that now, understanding that as a spiritual leader you will need to maintain purity and a faithful relationship with God. There are a lot of people doing Christ "stuff" and don't have Christ in their lives, living with no Holy Spirit. As a spiritual leader, you must have your life straight with Christ: committed to the will of God, following the guidance of the Holy Spirit, and living a life following the Word of God.

Key #7: Get Married

Nowadays, the institute of marriage is constantly being threatened by the world's desire to reinterpret its definition. People would rather date than marriage because they don't want the responsibility of ownership. However, God was very clear when he defined marriage as the Gospel covenant between Christ and believers. Christ is the bridegroom, and the church is the bride. In the parable found in Matthew 22, the king (father) is God and Jesus is the son. Two invitations were sent out. The first was sent long before the celebration so that people would have plenty of time to prepare for the banquet. After much time, a second invitation was sent to announce that the banquet was ready and that their attendance was now requested.

The plea of this verse undoubtedly portrays the ministry of John the Baptist (Matthew 3:1-3), Jesus (Matthew 4:17) and the disciples (Matthew 10:5-7). The guests are bidden to the wedding. In a Biblical sense, an invitation is sent to all who are within hearing of the joyful sound of the Gospel. No one is excluded but those who exclude themselves. The invitees "made light of it," meaning, they did not care to attend. In essence, those invited were so preoccupied with the here and now that they did not desire to hear about God's kingdom.

When the king saw that the invitees were slack in attending this event, he sent forth other servants: "Behold, the dinner is prepared, the oxen and the fatlings are killed, and all things are ready." Pardon is ready, peace is ready, comfort is ready, the promises are ready, and heaven is ready to receive us at last! Think about it. All this is ready; and shall we be unprepared? If all this preparation is made for us, is there any room to doubt our welcome? The reason why sinners don't seek salvation and come to Christ is not because they can't. It's because they won't. Sinners don't believe the "marriage" is an important event. They believe that they can have the same "wedding reception feast" at home. The sinners made light of attending this wedding because they don't consider this event a priority.

None turned their back on the feast, but they all gave some plausible excuse for not wanting to attend. While this parable was told thousands of years ago, the Scriptures in Matthew 22:8-9 describe the present times.

God is looking for a generation of leaders. But nobody wants to be committed nor convicted.

Because the king couldn't find spiritual leaders, he got natural leaders to do what the spiritual leaders are supposed to be doing. But few have chosen to wear the wedding garment and the garment of responsibility. Leadership is that you have taken off some stuff and put on other things that require responsibility and commitment.

Today's leaders experience the same disappointment. Meetings are called and the leaders are taken for granted. Some show up, others don't. Some call with plausible excuses, others don't even bother to call. The wedding (or kingdom) is our future. And the world, described by Christ as "many as you find" is being invited to participate in that future Earthly kingdom, which had been promised to Israel (Matthew 22: I 0). Both "bad and good" [people] probably refers to Jews and Gentiles. Those two groups include people who are morally evil and morally good.

God is calling for it all: everything you have. He is demanding a total commitment. He is demanding a marriage with you. If you are going to be a new generation of leaders, your commitment to God, to the vision of the pastor, and to your leadership assignment has to be one of marriage, owning this call on your life and working to complete it at all costs. The leadership responsibility on your life and the call on your life require a fulltime ownership of your role.

Regardless of their condition or preparation, people need to respond to the Gospel. More importantly, one group respond to the invitation even though it was a short notice, while those who had received special invitations had spurned the king's bidding (Matthew 22:11). The Bible says that one individual failed to prepare himself for the wedding before he arrived. The 19th Chapter of Revelations describes the formal preparation that must take place prior to attending the "lamb's wedding" with Christ. In Revelations 19:8, the garment of fine linen worn by the lamb's bride represents the righteous deed of the saints.

The unprepared man who attended the wedding had ignored a basic obligation placed on him when he accepted the king's gracious invitation to the feast: The guest was supposed to wear clean clothes. To attend a wedding banquet unprepared or in soiled clothing was considered an insult. In this parable, the garment most likely refers to the righteousness of Christ that he so graciously provided for us all through His death. To refuse to wear the garment of righteousness would mean a refusal of Christ's sacrifice. Or, an example of arrogance in belief that the "garment" was somehow not needed. Because this man was not prepared, the king declared him unworthy. His refusal to dress for the occasion resulted in the man being sent out of the banquet hall and into the "outer darkness"—a dense area that was farther away than the immediate darkness next to the banquet hall. For unbelievers, outer darkness refers to a place of suffering or Gahanna, the place of burning that has a furnace of fire (Matthew 22:31).

During the wedding feast, the king (God) was present to bid all of his guests. Let this be a warning to us against hypocrisy. God is a witness to all things. The hypocrite (unprepared guest) was never discovered to be without proper wedding attire until the king came in to greet the guests. It is God's will to know who is sound-at-heart in his profession. It is also the pastor's role to reprimand those who are in error. As humans, we can deceive one another but God cannot be deceived. As soon as God arrived and saw the unprepared guest, God kept his eye upon the deceiver.

There is no hope of being hid in a crowd from the arrest of justice. After all, the guest wasn't wearing a wedding garment nor did he even wear suitable clean clothing. It the Gospel represents the wedding feast, then the wedding garment is an example of a willingness of the heart, which is a course of life agreeable to the Gospel. This man was not naked or in rags: He was wearing some type of raiment. Only those who put on (accept) the Lord Jesus have dressed in the heavenly wedding garment.

Clearly, many are called to the wedding feast, but few have chosen to wear the wedding garment.

However, believers dressed for the wedding feast will shine as the sun in the kingdom of the Father. If you want to enter Christ's banquet, you must put on the "righteousness He gave us." In essence, as a spiritual leader, you must stay prepared at all times. You can learn from our peers as you pass time with other leaders and your pastor so that when the "invitation" comes, you will be prepared (Ephesians 4:24, Colossians 3:10).

In this instance, the phrase "children of the kingdom" refers to the unrepentant Jews who thought that because of their ancestry, they had automatic entrance into the kingdom of God. The Jews thought they were first to enter the kingdom but this parable by Jesus serves as a warning to them that they could be last. And those who thought themselves last, such as sinners, publicans and prostitutes, have the opportunity to be first, if they exercise faith in God (Matthew 21:31). Remember leaders, there's always someone waiting in the wings to take your place. So, if you're committed, stay that way and teach others as you go along.

Throughout the Bible as well as church history, spiritual covenants have been made between people in order for mutual edification and accountability. The most critical part of a marriage ceremony is when the man and woman exchange vows. Before witnesses and God, the bride and groom make certain promises to one another. This covenant between them is the essence of the marriage. In the same way, I believe the essence of church leadership is contained in the willingness to commit to a membership covenant and to work in a leadership position. This is one of the most important elements to relay to a new leader.

As leaders engaged in a marriage to God and their church, we should accomplish these four requirements to be in leadership:

1. Make a personal profession of Christ as Lord and Savior.
2. Be baptized by immersion as a public symbol of one's faith.
3. Participate regularly in leadership training and complete leadership tasks.

4. Sign a commitment contract to abide by your ministry's membership covenant.

5. As leaders, we commit to God to:
   1. Protect the unity of my church by acting in love toward other members, by refusing to gossip, and by following the head leadership. "So let us concentrate on the things which make for harmony and on the growth of our fellowship together." (Romans 15:19).
   2. Have a sincere love for your fellow believers: love one another earnestly with all your hearts (1 Peter 1:22).
   3. Speak in a manner that moves followers toward positive spiritual growth. "Do not let any unwholesome talk come out of your mouth, but only what is helpful for building others up according to their needs," (Ephesians 4:29).
   4. Obey your leaders and submit to their authority. They keep watch over you as men who must give an account to God. "Obey them so that their work will be a joy - not a burden - for that would be no advantage to you," (Hebrews 13:17). As a dynamic leader, you should also commit to share the responsibility of your church by praying for its growth, inviting the un-churched to attend, and by warmly welcoming those who visit. Consider I Thessalonians 1:2 (NKJV), *"To* the church, we always thank God for you and pray for you constantly." And

Jesus said unto the servant, "Go out to the roads and country lanes, and urge the people there to come so my house will be full," (Luke 14:23, NIV). Thus, you should warmly welcome each other into the church just as Christ has warmly welcomed you. Then, God will be glorified (Romans 15:7). God-appointed leaders shall serve the ministry of the church by discovering gifts and talents, skillfully equipped to serve pastors and operate with a servant's heart. In I Peter 4: 10 (PH), the mandate states, "Serve one another with the particular gifts God has given each of you." Ephesians 4:11-12 (NKJV) further explains a leader's gifts, "God gave...some to be pastors and teachers to prepare God's people for works of ministry, so that the body of Christ may be built up." You are to have the same subservient attitude of Christ (Philippians 2:3-4).

5. Remain in covenant marriage agree to support the testimony of their church by attending faithfully, living a Godly life and giving regularly. Hebrews 10:25 (NKJV) advises, "Let us not give up the habit of meeting together...but let us encourage one another." As the bride, you are to remain faithful in your marriage to Christ. "But whatever happens, make sure that your everyday life is worthy of the gospel of Christ." (Philippians I:27). By monetarily participating in the

covenant, you are to follow 1 Corinthians 16:2 (NKJV) which states, "Each one of you, on the first day of each week, should set aside a specific sum of money in proportion to what you have earned and use it for the offering." Remember, "A tenth of all your produce is the Lord's, and it is holy," (Leviticus 27:30, NKJV). The Bible is the inspired, inerrant word of God. And yet, why is it that so few read it? If God is a prayer-answering God (and He is), and if He meant for us to ask, seek and knock, then why is so little praying going on? Why do so many pastors have to beg and plead for members to give in the offerings for fear that church budgets will not be met and bills will not be paid? Statistics state that 40 percent of pastors quit after ten years and 50 percent quit after five years. This is sad! Leaders must be accountable.

There is no concrete answer to all of these questions, but there is spiritual answer that is tragically simple: many of God's people have never made a commitment to Him!

Deciding to act on your emotions about Jesus is vastly different from making a commitment to Him. Consider the story of Ananias and Sapphira in Acts 5. The couple made a commitment but they didn't follow through to its completion. In verse four of that chapter, the Scriptures state that the couple didn't lie to man. No, their tragic error was the lie they told to God. They didn't commit and entrust themselves to Him. Instead, they worked a scheme and lied. The result was death for them. As a God-appointed leader, you must marry God. When you marry Him, then you commit and entrust your life to Him. In this way, you make a lifelong decision to do it His way, which is the only way! Leadership is for life.

CHALLENGE

Now is the time to evaluate if you are prepared to marry God as a leader. Have you begun talking to your family about the sacrifice they and you will have to make as you walk in your calling? Have you talked with your spouse and let them know that this is something you have to do? True "armor bearing" is carrying the load that your Bishop is carrying. Are you prepared to change your source of income to follow your pastor and the vision of your church? Can you change things around and make the adjustments to lead? You may play ball every night but you now adjust your schedule to lead and serve the church? You have to prepare yourself and be organized to travel with your pastor and still take care of your family and responsibilities. You are marrying leadership and have to make time to pray, fast, check yourself to walking in God's authority and not your own. Can you make these adjustments? List ways that you will see your life adjusting as you marry leadership.

Key #8: Bathe in Obedience

As successful leaders, we must be obedient because everything falls under obedience.

Are you blessed in everything you do? Or, are you broke, busted and disgusted? Which of the two passages below best describes your life?

And it shall come to pass, if thou shalt hearken diligently unto the voice of the Lord thy God, to observe and to do all his commandments which I command this day, that the Lord thy God will set thee on high above all nations of the Earth; and all these blessings shall come on thee, and overtake thee; if thou shalt hearken unto the voice of the Lord thy God. Blessed shalt thou be in the city, and blessed shalt thou be in the field. Blessed shall be the fruit of thy body, and the fruit of thy ground, and the fruit of thy cattle, the increase of thy kin, and the flocks of thy sheep. Blessed shall be thy basket and thy store. Blessed shalt thou be when thou comest in, and blessed shalt thou be when thou goest out. The Lord shall cause thine enemies that rise up against thee to be smitten before thy face: they shall come out against thee one way, and flee before thee in thy storehouses, and in all that thou settest thine hand unto; and he shall bless thee in the land which the Lord thy God giveth thee (Deuteronomy 28:1-8).

OR

But it shall come to pass, if thou wilt not hearken unto the voice of the Lord thy God, to observe to do all His commandments and his statues which I command thee this day; that all these curses shall come upon thee, and overtake thee: cursed shalt thou be in the city, and cursed shalt thou be in the field. Cursed shall be thy basket and thy store. Cursed shall be the fruit of thy body, and thy fruit of thy land, the increase of thy kin, and the flocks of thy sheep. Cursed shalt thou be when thou comest in, and cursed shalt thou be when thou goest out (Deuteronomy 28:15-19).

As exceptional leaders, we must be obedient because everything falls on us. The Bible is very clear on the fact that there is a curse on this world. The ultimate curse is spiritual death, but the curse doesn't stop there. This blight includes sickness, poverty, and second death (endless troubles). The curse also leads to division of families and wasted resources. It destroys hopes and kills dreams. The curse is the domain of the devil.

The Bible also makes it apparent that freedom from this curse is possible!

Jesus Christ came to give us life, and life that is more abundant (John 10: 10). When we trust Him as Savior and give our life to Him, He redeems us from the curse of spiritual death. "*Christ hath redeemed us from the curse of the law, being made a curse for us; for it is written cursed is everyone that hangeth on a tree.*" (Galatians 3:13-14). His death on the cross paid the price for sin and bought us out of slavery and bondage to sin. As we commit our life to Him, making Him the Lord of our lives, His blessings follow after us and overtake us. *"That the blessing of Abraham might come on the Gentiles through Jesus Christ; that we might receive the promise of the spirit through faith"* (Galatians 3:14).

Let me make it clear once more:

The Blessings of Christ	The Curses of the Devil
Spiritual Life and Eternal Life	Spiritual Death
Health and Wholeness	Sickness and Disease
Love	Hate, Anger, Rebellion
Joy	Discouragement
Peace	Depression
Prosperity	Frustration/Worry/Fear
Unity in Families and Friendships	Poverty
	Divorce/Separation
Hopes and Dreams	Division
	Despair and Futility

Which way do you want to live? What is your heart's desire?

Every person I know would choose to live on the "Blessings of Christ" side! What are the conditions God places as a deciding factor about how a person will live? Read again the opening line of Deuteronomy 8:1 which states, "And it shall come to pass, if thou shalt hearken diligently to the voice of the Lord thy God, to observe and to do all his commandments." Hearing God's commandments and then observing and keeping God's commandments—that's the two-part condition places on us if we are to live a life of blessing!

What does it mean to "hearken diligently" to the voice of God? It means to seek out the voice of God who doesn't speak haphazardly. He doesn't speak from heaven through a huge megaphone. If a person is going to hear the voice of God, he must seek to hear the voice of God. He must go where God's word is being proclaimed. He must go to the Scriptures. He must make an effort to hear. The number one choice that we must make is a decision to put God first and to diligently seek Him and seek to hear His voice. If you truly put the Lord first, then nothing can keep you from blessings. The blessings are yours! People may not like you as a leader, but they won't be able to resist blessing you. Circumstances may line up against you but they won't be able to defeat you or to stop the flow of God's blessings. People may reject you, criticize you, or do their best to harm your reputation. But, they won't be able to overcome the blessings of God in your life.

If you are in the right position with God, nothing, nothing, nothing, absolutely nothing can keep you from being blessed. The only way you can find yourself in the "cursed" column of life is if you choose to disobey God. The devil knows this. That's why he spends so much time and effort to try to tempt you to disobey. That's why he does his utmost to get you to make bad choices when it comes to obeying God's commandments. That's why the enemy does whatever he can to keep you from seeking after God.

Think back over the parable of the prodigal son, which might also be called the parable of the loving father. Jesus told the story of a young man, who demanded his inheritance from his father before the father's death, then took that inheritance and squandered it. If you read this parable closely, you will see that although this young man was obviously rebellious and jealous, he didn't get into trouble until after he left his father's covering. As a leader, you must be able to recognize this fact, and understand how the young man became vulnerable and landed on the devil's turf.

When the boy left home, trouble hounded him and camped on his doorstep. Once the young man in the parable comes to his right spiritual senses and returns home, he again puts himself under his father's covering. At home, the young man received blessings and a full restoration of his role as a son including full provision and protection (Luke 15:11-32).

Essentially, this parable is about our relationship with our heavenly Father. Jesus made it very obvious that as long as we are in an obedient relationship with God the Father, then we will experience the fullness of the Father's blessings. It's when we willfully choose to walk away in disobedience that we experience the curse of the devil.

As long as we maintain a close, obedient and faithful covenant with the Lord, the devil can't touch us. Can you begin to understand why the devil will try to keep a person from attending church? Can you see why the devil will attempt to prevent a person from opening his Bible, getting on his knees to pray and stop him from putting his tithe into the offering? If you stop obeying the Lord, if you stop seeking Him and stop looking to hear His voice, then you open yourself up to direct assault from the devil. When you're open to the enemy's attack, then you're open to a life marked by curses not blessings. The choice is yours. The Bible clearly defines your options.

In Deuteronomy 30:19-20, the Scriptures explain that if you put God first and foremost, you will succeed in all things. But, if you put anything before God, then everything you touch will ultimately fail. It's just that clear cut; and it's not easy. It's not easy to make the right decisions. There's a price to pay for obedience. Everyday can seem like a test. You may find that every circumstance seems to go wrong when you start walking right. The good news is that God walks through the testing times with you. He gives you strength as you make correct decisions. He turns them around, and in the end, if you put all your life in God's hand, He causes you to experience blessings.

Obey God's statues. God's word declares that blessings are yours if we "observe" and "do" all the commandments of God. At times, the Bible talks about obeying God's statues. What is the difference between a commandment and a statue? In technical terms, a commandment is a statement of overriding principal and law. A statue is a rule that is very practical and very direct.

God's expectations for order in our lives are listed in the Ten Commandments. The first four of the commandments spell out our relationship with God (Exodus 20: 1-17). We are to put God first, have no idols, refrain from taking the Lord's name in vain, and keep the Sabbath. The next six commandments define our relationship with others. We are to honor our parents. We must not kill or covet our neighbor's possessions and so forth.

The Ten Commandments as well as all of the other commandments direct us to the two "great commandments" taught by Jesus (Matthew 22:37-40). The two special commandments tell us how to love God with our whole heart, soul and mind. The laws also tell us how to love others. Throughout the Bible, we find repeated passages that point us to the truth that if a person doesn't put the Lord in his life, and if he doesn't "love God with his whole heart, soul and mind," then he is in disobedience. By operating in disobedience, the person isn't following the first commandment.

You will also find several passages in the Bible regarding the second great commandment with respect to love. If a person doesn't love others as himself, then he is in disobedience. The tithe, for example, is a very concrete and specific statue that lets us know if we are truly loving God and faithfully seeking to obey Him. Again, if you do not treat God with the love that He expects and leave from under His covering, then curses will come upon you as a leader.

The Reason for a Curse

God doesn't allow a curse in your life because He's mad at you. The truth is that He loves you enough to get your attention and try to convince you to change your mind. The purpose of the "curse" is for you to change your life and choose obedience! "How can I tell if my finances are cursed," you ask? A curse often displays itself in the following ways:

- You can never get ahead. You live from paycheck to paycheck and never seem to have anything when an emergency comes along
- Your materials possessions appear less than other people with equal financial stature. You find that you frequently look at other people and say, "They seem lucky" because they are able to afford things you can't

afford even though they work where you work and earn the same pay.
- You experience simultaneous setbacks. Your roof springs a leak. The car breaks down and the dog runs away. You wring your hands and feel as if you're being punished.

If you confess to being a Christian and claim to love God, but you frequently make excuses about obeying "certain parts" of the Bible, then you are living under a curse. If you find that you are continually questioning why you are broke, you are experiencing a curse. If you find that you have a great feeling of dissatisfaction all the time about money, bills and your financial stature, then you are living under a curse. As leaders, we cannot afford to live under a curse. We must always be in position to receive and be a blessing to others. We do this to edify and build the church.

CHALLENGE

Stand in the mirror and say to yourself, "I have lived under a curse and today the curse stops. I give myself to being obedient to God and to live with a renewed mind. I walk in the knowledge that I have been cursed because I have not walked in the instruction and call that You have placed in me and chose for me. I repent for not obeying the call on my life and will now walk in the call faithfully, obediently, and with fear of the Lord and His authority over my life and my responsibility. Today, I will live as an obedient spiritual leader, fasting, praying, hearing the voice of God, sacrificing, believing the promises of Mark 10:29, and knowing that the sacrifice and obedience brings blessings on me and those I lead."

Note how this confession and statement of faith frees you. Take this new feeling of calmness and safety. It should usher you into prayer time where you can hear from God, clearly.

Key #9: Release Your Anointing

In the book of John, we are introduced to a woman destined to become a great leader. Jesus was in Bethany at the home of Lazarus just completing supper when a momentous event occurred. "Then took Martha pound of ointment of spikenard, very costly, and anointed the feet of Jesus, and wiped his feet with her hair: and the house was filled with the odour of the anointment," (John 12:3). Mary had a revelation that made a revolution into the kingdom of God.

As the Scriptures state, the oil was costly and this woman of meager means chose to anoint her Savior versus make a profit from selling the oil. In essence, she chose to give her most precious gift in order to declare her love for God. Many of us believe that we are positioned in the body of Christ merely to receive. I believe the theory is based on our background and our feelings of self-worth after having "earned" our way to the top. After working extremely hard and experiencing a great deal of tribulation, many expect to be the receiver when God sends His anointing out to the fold.

It is pivotal that we not only hear the Word, but must receive the Word in order for the Word to transform our lives. Ironically, as some have received the word they also have lost sight of purpose in the Kingdom. As effective leaders, we have become students of the Word. However, every original Christian can understand and pick-up any translation of the Word and receive revelation. Our job is to provide accurate translation of the Word and true guidance to followers.

Years ago, revelation was only handed out to a few. But because we are now living in the Age of Information, the world is increasing in knowledge. Thus, revelation also continues to increase in the body of Christ. Revelation comes when we receive the knowledge of God, which provides insight into our daily walk. Not only do you receive a few mere thoughts from God, but you also receive an impartation from Him. The Apostle Peter said that by these divine promises we become as "partakers" of His divine nature and God then sends glory waves of revelation!

Remember, God has purpose in mind. His purpose is that we become a partaker of His divine nature so that we do more than just sit in church and receive knowledge for the sake of knowledge. You should never want to be in a position of forever learning, but never coming into the knowledge of the truth of God. The truth: You cannot remain a spectator in the house of God ready to receive another revelation. Instead, God will take you to a place where you can receive impartation that will bring a revelation.

When we as leaders receive an impartation, we become "Kingdom participators." It's "Kingdom Time!" We have always thought that the preachers, teachers, prophets, evangelists and apostles live in the Kingdom to do the work of the ministry. The five-fold comes to give us a revelation so we can do the work of the ministry. We think that ministry workers are the teachers, and the preachers assigned to expose and discern the work of God. But, it's time for you to get to work.

It's time that you release the anointing that God has imparted inside of you. When you become born again and filled with the Spirit of God, you become anointed! As a leader, you may not have figured out what your special anointing is but you definitely have an anointing. The enemy may make you feel like you don't. He is only trying to hold you hostage: He wants to incarcerate your soul and make you feel like you don't qualify to have any kind of anointing or blessing from God. The enemy will even make you feel like the best that you can do in the house of God is to be faithful, bring your tithes and offerings, and offer God praise.

But God has much more than that in store for you. The real deal is that we have been majoring in trying to graduate instead of concerning ourselves with the elementary things of God. We get stuck on learning the basic foundation of the Word. Then, we reach the place where we think we have now arrived. However, God is taking us to higher ground: to the point where we are so full of His Word that we no longer will look through the eyes of zeal and wish and hope. Then, you will reach the point where you can be used by God!

CHALLENGE

When God places His hand on you to do a task that is easy—second nature—for you, this is your anointing. Someone else would get tired but you will never get tired of doing the thing God put in you to do. He shows you an easy way of doing it. The burden is in you to do it. Releasing it is doing it. Again, It is going to cost you a lot. Understanding this, what is your anointing? What has God made room for you to do? What is that you have been gifted by God to do that only you can do? Remember, according to Prov. 18:16, your gift will make room for you and bring you before great men. If you have not followed the challenges in previous chapters, stop now and work back through the challenges. Once you have done them all, honestly review your response in light of what you now understand your anointing and call to be. What will you change about your level of obedience, prayer, fasting, and commitment in light of what you now have confirmed to be your anointing?

Key #10: Keep the Fire Burning

Leviticus 6:8-13 reveals how Moses was ordered by God to assign Aaron and his sons as keepers of the Holy fire. They were to follow the law of the burn offering, "*because of the burning upon the altar all night unto the morning, and the fire of the altar shall be burning in it.* "(Leviticus 6:9). During Biblical times, the Holy fire on the altar had to keep burning because God lit the fire. The flames represented God's continual presence in the sacrificial system. It showed the people that only by God's gracious favor could their sacrifices by acceptable. Today, God's fire remains present in each believer's life. God lights the fire when the Holy Spirit comes to live in us. God tends to the flames so that we will grow in grace as we walk with Him. When you are aware that God lives in you and that the fire is burning, then you will have confidence to go to Him for forgiveness and restoration. You can carry out your work with strength.

The altar is the place of sacrifice. At the altar, natural, earthly things that hinder your walk with God are consumed by the fire of God. You become a "living sacrifice" at the altar. As efficient leaders, we must become a living sacrifice. In Romans 12:1-3, the Apostle Paul says that you must wash and undergo the "fire of consecration" to qualify as a leader in the ministry. This burning transformation is your opportunity to operate using the newly-learned leadership ideas, attitude and skills. You must lay down your life to embrace God's perfect will. Everything within you that doesn't stand up to God's perfect plan will be burned. Those inequalities are set on fire and consumed in the spirit. That's why in Matthew 3:11, John says that Jesus will baptize you with the Holy Spirit and with fire.

The baptism of the Holy Spirit brings with it a new spiritual sensitivity—one that is multi-functional. Just as we become increasingly aware of God's inner presence, we also gain insight on the presence of sin. This amplified sensitivity to sin is matched by a desire for personal holiness. But while the spirit is willing, the flesh is often weak. Potentially, you die to the old nature when you are born again. *"We know that our old self was crucified with Him so that the sinful body might be destroyed and we might no longer be enslaved to sin.*" (Romans 6:6, *NKJV*).

Many may experience immediate deliverance from a particular illness, addiction or personal weakness as a result of being baptized in the Holy Spirit. Some feel new and unmistakable joy and power. Yet for all, the battle against the "old man" continues to be waged in other areas of life. THERE IS NO SUCH THING AS INSTANT HOLINESS!!

The crucifixion of the old man, which begins with the rebirth and is intensified by the baptism in the Holy Spirit, is a long and arduous process. Scholars may be right when they claim that this purging is the "fire" John the Baptist spoke of when he said Jesus would baptize with the Holy Ghost and with fire. We would be less than honest to claim that such an inflow of spiritual power has no crucifying element. It does!

You must always remember that once you confess and declare that you believe the works of Christ and what He has done in your life, then every work of the Lord in your life shall be tried by fire. More importantly, I Corinthians 3:12-15 says that some works are made of straw, and others are made of wood. But only that which endures the fire will qualify to be used of God. As leaders, we must know that we will go through the fire and must endure.

For example, gold jewelry is forged by being placed in fire. The goldsmith's purpose for heating the metal is to draw the impurities and black tar particles to the surface. Then, the goldsmith pulls the gold out of the fire, scrapes off the impurities and foreign particles, and puts the gold back into the fire. This process is repeated several times until the goldsmith has reached the deepest interior of that lump of gold. During this process, any particles that would cause this piece of jewelry not to shine or be appraised as pure gold are burned off thus increasing the gold's value.

God operates in our lives using this same purifying method. When you allow God to put you "in the fire" or in fiery situations, you are agreeing with everything He is working through you. You are being cleansed from impurities that would hinder you from becoming a most valuable resource to Him and His work. Jesus has already perfected the fire. Meaning, He has already tempered the flame to facilitate each and every person that will enter. No two people experience the same trial. No one goes through the same fire.

The fire will not consume the part of you that He desires to use. This is not a destructive flame. It is a constructive one. Although this fire burns away bad elements, it also allows that which remains to be formed and shaped until it adheres completely to His image. God will be with you, just as He was with Shadrach, Meschach and Abednego when they were thrown into the fiery furnace (Daniel 3:24-25).

In order to keep the flames lit, wood must be placed in the fire every day. We are the wood. The wood represents humanity and whenever humanity is involved, there are limitations. The altar is where God atoned for the limitations of man through the shedding of blood. In ancient Israel, priests sacrificed animals at this altar. Jesus became the final sacrificial lamb (Isaiah 53:5-7). He was placed upon the wood of sacrifice. He went under the fire, died on the cross and He didn't open His mouth in objection.

When you die to the flesh in sacrifice, the fires enable you to rise up in the Spirit and walk into the Holy place. God is saying the fire must never go out. You must daily put yourself in the fire. If you don't put your flesh on the altar and offer yourself up as a sacrifice, then you will be limited to what you can do for Him. Purifying the flesh is the most important act of obedience. What is your flesh? It is everything you think and feel except that which is a result of the will of God and His Word within you.

Sacrifice always comes before service. Many people serve God in the sanctuary preaching, praying, prophesying and laying on hands. But, they haven't truly been on fire. They haven't stopped at the place of sacrifice and given everything to God.

Unfortunately, they are still controlled by their own will. In the Garden of Gethsemane, Jesus prayed until *"His sweat became like great clots of blood dropping."* (Luke 22:44).

He laid down His will to put it in the fire. *"Father, if you are willing, remove this cup from me, yet not my will, but always yours be done"* (Luke 22:42, NKJV).

At this moment in the realm of the Spirit, Jesus had made it to the fire. He lay before God and said, "In my flesh, I don't want to do this. I can't do this ...nevertheless.. .I want what you want. I'm not going to let the limitations of my flesh keep me from the supernatural operation of my spirit."

God requires us to lay ourselves on the altar daily and say, "Whatever doesn't please you, Lord, burn it up. Consume my will, desires, and emotions—anything that doesn't live up to Your will." We are the wood that keeps God's eternal fire burning on the altar. In other words, the fire will reflect your level of sacrifice on the brazen altar.

Your submitted life help keeps the fire burning. If you don't keep yourself on the altar like fresh wood that is laid upon it daily, then the fire will go out. If this happens, you won't have an illumination of God's word in the hard places as well as in the Holy places. If you jump off the fire too soon, you will be in danger. Leviticus 6:9 indicates that God burned not only the things that can be seen, but also the things in the dark, hidden places.

Don't jump off the altar while your sins and limitations are still being consumed by fire. If you jump off too soon, not only could you fall back into sin, but your fire could also go out. If you fall, get up and start again. The Bible says that when we fall, we have to do our "first works over again," according to Revelations 2:5. Jesus told us to work "while it is day for when the night cometh, no man can work" (John 9:4, NKJV). You can't move forward when you are in spiritual darkness. You can't see where you are going! Stay in the fire until God takes you out.

CHALLENGE

You cannot do the work of a spiritual leader without the fire of the Holy Ghost. To be able to effectively become a problem solver for your pastor and lead a ministry without the proper sleep, you need the Holy Ghost. It will burn off those sinful things in your life. It will keep you pure. It will keep you trustworthy. Remember, the pastor and God are trusting you with responsibility. A lot of things will try to distract you, but the Holy Ghost will burn off what will distract you. It's the fire of the Holy Ghost that burns envy, jealousy, animosity off of you so you don't have to serve. It's the fire of the Holy Ghost that keeps your heart right. Keep the fire burning so you can keep your heart pure. The only way you can serve in leadership is with a pure heart. This challenge involves keeping the fire burning, kindling close. Keep it burning in your life. You don't want your good to be spoken evil of. You can never flow and be the follower of your leader with envy. You have to do it early on so that when these things come and your heart can help.

You cannot walk in this without the Holy Spirit. It is a gift from God. He is the inward dwelling of God in you. You have to have the Holy Spirit living in you. The evidence of Holy Ghost is speaking in tongues and prophesies. It's not a feeling; it's a knowing. In order to keep it burning, there must be quality time together to kindle the fire. Document the number of hours and days when you are spending quality and intimate time in prayer and conversation with God, meditating on His word, or resting and communing with the Holy Spirit.

Key #11: Decide to Persevere

And he said, Let me go, for the day breaketh. And he said, I will not let thee go, except thou bless me.

(Genesis 32:26)*.*

To persevere means to remain constant with force—despite the opposing force (or obstacle). Oftentimes, perseverance requires supernatural strength—power that flows down from God. In the case of Jacob and his battle with the angel, Jacob wrestled valiantly for hours according to Genesis 32:24. The picture of Jacob wrestling the angel until daybreak demonstrates the power of perseverance in producing spiritual success.

Jacob said, "I will not let you go." He made a decision to persevere—hold on until you bless me. The angel renamed him "Prince of God" and a common drifter is perseverance! All Biblical figures have an understanding of perseverance such as Solomon, who in all his wisdom writes, 'The righteous are bold as a lion," (Proverbs 28:1). Jesus Christ, the son of God, is referred to as "the Lion of the tribe of Judah" in Revelation 5:5. God's people are bold, fearless fighters. We are not on Earth to compromise with evil: We are here to conquer evil.

Christ is the most powerful fighter and He had to persevere a great deal. "Looking unto Jesus, the author and finisher of our faith, who for the joy that was set before him endured the cross," (Hebrews 12:2, NKJV). Calvary wasn't a picnic ground: It was "ground zero" in the universal war zone! Calvary was heaven's high water mark for perseverance! How can you tell who is a follower of Christ? Not by the person's speech.

People can talk the talk, but don't walk the walk. Perseverance is part of the Christian life. The Bible is a book of perseverance. The portrait of perseverance is exemplified when you consider Noah and his work to build the ark. For 120 years, Noah endured all humanity laughing at him. His generation had never seen rain. Yet, perseverance put the animals on a gigantic boat. Perseverance placed Noah's wife and children on the boat with blue skies and 72-degree weather. Perseverance is a fire in your bones that will carry you through ridicule, rejection and reversal. Perseverance does not need public approval. And, perseverance couldn't care less about being politically correct. Perseverance in faith says, "Mountain get out of my way! Nothing is impossible to them that believe," according to Matthew 17:20.

You stick with it knowing, "If God be for you, who can be against you," (Romans 8:31). "The victory is ours through Christ the Lord," (I Corinthians 15:37). And know that, "Faith is the victory that overcomes the world," (I John 5:4).

There is nothing half-hearted or lukewarm about perseverance. It's bold. It's daring. It's fearless. Perseverance is Nehemiah rebuilding the walls of Jerusalem when powerful men organized a slander campaign to stop the building project. When defamation of character could not stop him, the antagonists threatened to kill him.

Nehemiah passed out swords to half his men and gave bricks to the other half. He made it clear that he was ready to fight to the end. We as leaders also have to act in this valiant manner. The wall was rebuilt to the glory of God through the power of perseverance. The Apostle Paul exemplified the power of perseverance as he lived his life spreading the Gospel. Many times he writes that he was, "Persecuted, but not forsaken; cast down, but not destroyed," (2 Corinthians 4:8-9).

The night before Paul's head was chopped off; the Apostle of perseverance again put his pen to parchment in a dim glow of the candle and wrote, "I have fought a good fight, I have finished my course, I have kept the faith: Henceforth there is laid up for me a crown of righteousness," (2 Timothy 4:7-8).

Have you been knocked down? Have you been betrayed by a dear friend? Have you experienced the death of a loved one? Are you fighting a deadly disease? Are you in a financial crisis? Leaders, rise! Get up! Get up now! You have the power to persevere.

Give up every idea of quitting...Now! It's always too soon to quit! The Bible does not say, "Those who begin well shall be saved." No, it says, "They who endure to the end shall be saved," (Matthew 24:13). The Apostle Paul said it well, "So we may boldly say: The Lord is my helper I will not fear. What can man do to me?" (Hebrews 13:6, *KJV*).

An over comer can make a definite decision—just as Jesus did in the Garden of Gethsemane. He knew all too well the torture that lay ahead and He naturally began by prayer (Luke 22:42). Perseverance is Jesus hanging on the cross—bleeding from His hands, head, side and feet. As a leader, you must look into your soul and decide you will not play the role of a coward. You must make a definite decision to endure. You will persevere—period! People who have perseverance, "Do it anyway!" Perseverance was simple: Those who persevere are the ones left standing when everyone else quits! If you are a son or daughter of God, then quitting the church is unthinkable!

Perseverance is Job attending the funeral of his ten children after losing his wealth, health, and listening to his wife who had a tongue sharp enough to clip a hedge. Remember her encouraging words? She advised Job, "Curse [God] and die!" (Job 2:9). Or, do you recall the words of Job's three dear friends who accused him of sinning? They accused him of folly, told him that God was chastening him and advised Job to repent. Yet, despite all these dear words, Job persevered. He said, "Though God slay me, I will come forth as pure gold."

As an anointed leader, you must dig within for that stick-to-itiveness. I will not quit! I will endure! It's too soon to quit. Finish what you start! All too often we find men who begin projects and then give up easily. Unfortunately, our generation lives in the era of instant gratification. We want it now. I can hear the voice of God saying, "But he who endures to the end shall be saved." Leaders, make a decision to persevere.

CHALLENGE

Every leader has to have a double dose of perseverance. There will be days your family isn't with you, days you don't have money, and you will have to push and go. That's a part of leadership. Are you going to go in difficult times. Learn how to get up after a fall. Can you go when you are embarrassed and talked about? Can you still serve as a leader and not let anyone know you are going through trouble. You can not stop.

Are you going to be able to go when it's hard? This is not the time to just say, "Sure, of course I can". If you are not making it to your area because you are going through something, you are not persevering. You can't say I'm not singing because I don't have the car or because of this or that. You can't complain about it. You have to serve. Take a moment and search honestly within yourself: can you push through?

Key #12: Work with the Team

And the Lord God said, It is not good that the man should be alone; I will make him a helpmeet for him (Genesis 2:18).

As you can see from the above Scripture, God knew that Adam needed help. Thus, he created Eve to be part of the team that would build the world. When Nehemiah attempted to rebuild the wall of Jerusalem, he quickly sought help from the Jews (priests, nobles, officials and citizens). In Nehemiah 2:17 *(NKJV)* he says, "Jerusalem lies in ruins, and its gates have been burned with fire. Come, let us build the wall of Jerusalem, and we will no longer be in disgrace."

We need other people if we are going to be successful in life because we were not created to fulfill our dreams alone. As we read in Genesis 2: 18 (KJV), God specifically said about His first creation, "It is not good for man to be alone." We need people to make it in life. Again, individual purposes are always fulfilled within a larger or corporate purpose. Therefore, it's important that we work with others to make our dreams a reality.

Remember Nehemiah? He was the one who had received the vision, but he had to go to other people to help him complete the vision. For any dream that you have, God has people divinely assigned and prepared to work with you. And, they will be a blessing to you. There will always be a need for positive people in your life. When you have a dream, that's the way it works. People will always be there waiting to help you. Therefore, if you have no dream, or, if you do not begin to act on it, then the people who are supposed to help you won't know where to find you. Remember, you are part of someone else's destiny.

Thus, you become like those with whom you spend time. Meaning, the principle of influence has a two-fold application. People can have a negative effect on us as well as a positive one. When you begin to act on your vision, it will stir up both those who want to help you and those who want to hinder you.

The Law of Association

The law of association states that you become like those with whom you spend time. We often underestimate other's influence in our lives. There are two words that most accurately describe influence: powerful and subtle. Often, you don't know you're being influenced until it's too late. Leaders, watch out. Whether you realize it or not, the influence of your associates has a powerful affect on if you will succeed or fail in life.

What we call peer pressure is simply this: *People* with we associate exercise their influence on us. Associates try to direct our lives in the way that they want us to go. We should stop telling young people that they alone have peer pressure. Adults undergo pressure too. You must be careful whom you allow to influence you or speak into your life. Your dream will either be encouraged or destroyed by others. There are two kinds of people in this world: You have supporters and antagonists. I have learned that people have the potential to create your environment. Your surroundings then determine your mindset, which then determines your future. Therefore, you must choose your friends wisely.

Select only those who are with you—not against you. "Show me your friends, and I'll show you your future," said Dr. Bill Cosby.

Questions of Influence

You should generally choose friends who are going in the same direction you are, and want to obtain the same goals so you can uplift one another. Ask yourself three questions when selecting a potential friend. First ask, "With whom am I spending time?" Who are you closest friends? Who are your confidantes? Secondly, "How does this person influence me?" In other words, what does this person have you listening to, reading, thinking or doing? Where does he have you going? What does he have you saying? How does he have you feeling? Does he have you settle instead of reaching higher? That last question is an important one because your friends can make you comfortable in your misery.

Most importantly, how is hanging around this person influencing your behavior?

Solomon said, "He who walks with the wise grows wise, but a companion of fools suffers harm," (proverbs 13:20). The New King James Version reads, "The companion of fools will be destroyed." My version of this philosophy is, "If you want to become a success, don't keep company with those who aren't going anywhere in life." Thirdly, ask yourself, "Is what other people are doing to me a good thing in relation to my dream?"

Visions and dreams awaken opposition. Nehemiah 4:1 (NKJV) says, "When Sanballat heard that we were rebuilding the wall, he became angry and was greatly incensed." People of vision have found that the minute they decide to fulfill their dreams, all their enemies seem to wake up. Again, as long as you're not doing anything about your vision, no one will bother you. If you start to move toward your vision, however, opposition arises.

It is an interesting phenomenon that certain people will become angry when you step out and start to do something that they have never accomplished. Friends and associates don't want you to break out of your situation because they don't want you to leave them behind. You need to get used to the idea that people may gossip about you and treat you with malice because of your vision. It's all part of the process! Oftentimes, jealousy and ridicule is proof that you're really accomplishing something with your life.

The potential for negative influences from family members in regard to vision is probably the reason why the Lord said to Abraham, "Leave your country, your people and your father's household and go to the land I show you," (Genesis 2:1, NKJV).

The Scripture doesn't say that Abraham's wife, Sarah, was present at the time, which was a good thing. Remember that later on, Sarah laughed with unbelief when God said she would have a child in her old, barren age. Joseph also had to leave his family before he could become what was essentially the prime minister of Egypt. Sometimes, we need to pull away from the influence of even those we love if we're going to follow our God-given visions. Many people want you to be what they desire—not what you were born to become. Often, those same friends end up limiting your growth.

Your passions have to be more powerful than the opposition of those around you. You must be clear about what you're going to do and persevere in finishing the task. Nehemiah faced this very situation (Nehemiah 4:2). Look at the question Sanballat was asking. When people are angry, they ask questions to discourage you. Verse three says, "Tobiah the Ammonite, who was at his side, said, "What they are building if even a fox climbed up on it, he would break down their wall of stones," (Nehemiah 4:3, NKJV). In other words, "Don't worry about them. This isn't going to work; it will soon come to nothing." Have you ever heard that before? Oh, don't worry about that new business.

When someone says a phrase like that, you just keep moving forward with your vision.

The reason some people may begin to hate you when you pursue your vision is that you are exposing their own lack of vision. There are toxic people in the world, and they will pollute your whole life if you let them.

Disassociation

Priority requires that there are people and places that you are going to have to disassociate yourself from if you're going to make it to your dreams. This fact shouldn't be taken lightly. Some people say that it doesn't really matter with whom they associate because they wouldn't want to hurt anyone by disassociating from them. Yet, Jesus said, "If the blind leads the blind, both will fall into a ditch," (Matthew 5:14, NKJV). He was telling us not to be foolishly following those who are spiritually blind. You have to disassociate yourself from people who aren't going anywhere and don't want to go anywhere in life. The sad thing is that some people literally sacrifice their dreams and their lives because they are afraid of facing conflict and disagreement with others. Don't be afraid to disassociate yourself from people who aren't right for you. Disassociation does not need to be confrontational. Sometimes, you can ease out of people's lives very quietly and very subtle - just as you eased into them. Disassociation is not an easy action to take. But it is a very important priority in life. Remember what Nehemiah said when his enemies tried to distract him from his vision. He says, I am carrying on a great project and cannot go down. Why should the work stop while I leave it and go down to you," (Nehemiah 6:3, NKJV).

Limited Association

The second concept that I have learned about making the dream work is to establish limited association. You may not want to completely determine how much time you will spend a person. However, you should spend major time with positive influences and minor time with negative influences. For those of you who are dating and becoming excited about your relationship, please take this information to heart. When you have a goal for your life, make sure that the person you are interested in is also interested in your goals.

Many people get married and then tell their spouses their goals. Often, their spouses say, "I really don't want that." Consider the question posed in Amos 3:3 (NKJV), "Can two walk together unless they are agreed?" That would be an extremely difficult walk. Jesus reinforced this theme when He said, "A house divided against itself will fall," (Luke **11:** 17, NKJV). Trust me, you don't want to be in a house that is divided. You must protect your mental environment. Here's how to do so. Stay away from bad situations. Paul quoted the adage in I Corinthians 15:33, which states, "Bad company corrupts good character," (NKJV). In other words, Paul was telling us, "Choose your company well."

Expanded Association

This is the most positive of the three concepts. Basically, you should expand your association. If you're going to be successful, you have to spend more time with the right people. Spend time with people who have the same philosophy and discipline that you possess.

Make sure that these influences are the same kind of people who exhibit the same or similar character traits. Such people are the persons with whom you want to expand your relationship.

Ask yourself the following questions. Who can help me toward my goal? Which person can I get close to and learn from? You should spend time with people of vision. When the angel Gabriel announced to Mary that she would become pregnant with Jesus, Mary asked, "How can I have a baby?" God's answer through Gabriel was that this pregnancy would occur through the power of the Holy Spirit.

Yet, notice what else the angel said. He mentioned that Elizabeth was pregnant with John the Baptists after she had been both barren and past the age of child-bearing.

It was as if God was saying, "Mary, to help you stay strong during this time, you need the faith-inspiring testimony of Elizabeth. She has her own miracle baby, and she's six months ahead of you." The Bible says that Mary left her family and went straight to Elizabeth's house to stay with her. Again, Mary disassociated herself from her own parents and siblings in order to expand her association with Elizabeth, her cousin.

CHALLENGE

Can you work well with others? This is something you passed or failed in elementary school. True leadership is inspiring others to do it. Leadership is not one person doing everything; it involves delegation. Leadership is you getting people to do things they did not realize they can do it. Create other people to do what you are doing. True leadership is finding successors so that you can continue to move forward. Get in your mind that you have to reinvent yourself.

You are fighting spirits of intimidation and jealousy and you have to guard yourself early as a leader to appreciate the gifts around you and let them not intimidate you.

Key #13: Take the Limits Off

Enlarge your house, build an addition; spread out your home! For you will soon be bursting at the seams; your descendants will take over other nations and live in their cities. Fear not: you will no longer live in shame. The shame of your youth and the sorrows of widowhood will be remembered no more.

For the Creator will be your husband. The Lord almighty is his name! He is your Redeemer, the Holy One of Israel, the God of all the Earth (Isaiah 54:2-4).

During Biblical times, to be childless was a woman's great shame and a disgrace. Families depended on children for survival, especially when the parents became elderly. Israel (Jerusalem) was unfruitful like a barren woman, but God would permit her to have many children and transform her mourning into singing. *"And thy seed shall be as the dust of the Earth, and thou shalt spread abroad to the west, and to the east, and to the north, and to the south, and in thee and in thy seed shall all the families of the Earth be blessed"* (Genesis 28:14, NKJV).

As a God-fearing leader, you are in line to receive a multitude of blessings. Proverbs 10:22 (NKJV) states, *"The blessing of the Lord, it maketh rich, and He addeth no sorrow with it."* This is a promise in the word of God, and it is personal. It is also a principle of faith. We call what we want into existence. We speak as though it has come to pass because we know that it already has in the heart of God, in the mind of God and in the plan of God. Through our confession or claim to receive the blessing, we are, in essence, agreeing with the word of God.

The term "confession" originates from the Greek phrase "home loggia" which means to say the same thing or as to say "in agreement with." We as leaders just choose by an act of our will not to look at our present state and call another into existence. We do it repetitiously—not hit and misses. Do you believe you are on God's heart? Do you think you are on God's heart when you have problems? Psalm 115:12-14 (NKJV) states, *"The Lord hath been mindful of us; he will bless us; he will bless your house. He will bless the house of Israel; He will bless the house of Aaron. He will bless them that fear the Lord, both small and great. The Lord shall increase you more and more, you and your children."* You are on God's mind because He wants you to step outside of your limitations. He wants you to live a life of abundance and increase.

You are not on God's mind because of any other reason than Him thinking about how He can increase His child. He is thinking, "How can I bless my child? How can I pour my blessing over my child?" According to Psalm 84:11, "The Lord God is your sun and shield, and He will endow you with grace and glory. The Scripture goes on to say, "No good thing will he withhold from them that walk uprightly."

When you love God, you are going to love His word. If you love His word, you are going to spend time meditating on the word of God. When you do that, the Bible says God is going to cause you to inherit true riches - not just money - the true stuff! You will receive what's called endurable wealth. According to Psalm 112:3 (NKJV), "*Wealth and riches shall be in his house: and his righteousness endureth forever.*" The Amplified Bible states, "*Prosperity and welfare are in his house, and righteousness endures forever.*"

Attention leaders! God wants you to prosper. No limits!

God is a God of abundance. John 10:10 (NKJV) says, "I am come that they might have life, and that they may have it more abundantly." That does not mean to have enough money to barely scrape by or to be one paycheck away from homelessness.

Abundance in God's terms means that you have enough to get your needs met and then some. Your portion is to enjoy life. It is good for me to have a good life. It is good for me to be able to walk in the store and say, "I want one of those and I want one of those and I want one of those!" That is my portion. Leaders, work on your portion. There is no limit to God's blessings!

CHALLENGE

Take off your restraints. God's going to please the leaders. Write what you are believing God for because its going to manifest because Hebrews 6:10. He is not unjust to forget your work and labor of love in that you have ministered to the saints and do ministry. God Is keeping good record and God Is going to give you blessing, creativity, winning ideas, open doors, shut doors, cause you to be on top and going higher because you have employed what is in this book. You work for the riches man in the universe. What you make happen for others with a pure heart, God is going to make it happen for you.

Key #14: Be Courageous

Courage is the bold, daring effort to overcome the uncertainty of the present as well as confront the disappointment and pain of the past with a dependence on God to passionately pursue the future. Courage is a human commodity that you must possess. It is a product of determination. According to the Bible, when God told Joshua to lead the children of Israel into the Promised Land, God repeatedly told Joshua to have courage enough to complete the journey. *"Be strong and of good courage: for unto this people shalt thou divide for an inheritance the land, which I sware unto their fathers to give them. Only be thou strong and very courageous, that thou mayest observe to do according to all the law, which Moses my servant commanded thee"* (Joshua 1:6, NKJV). Although

Joshua and the children of Israel had witnessed the power of God, they had to exercise courage and boldness in order to conquer obstacles and achieve God's plan for them.

When it comes to obtaining material wealth, financial prosperity and going to higher ground, you must possess an anointed level of boldness and courage. I trust that after reading this book you will be confident in your leadership potential, sustained in your salvation, assured of your anointing, and heading to higher ground. Once you understand this next verse and the real definition of the term "wealthy place," you will understand your purpose as a leader striving to reach Higher Ground. Incidentally, Higher Ground is also called your wealthy place. Psalm 66:12 (NKN) states, *"Thou hast caused men to ride over our heads; we went through fire and through water but thou broughtest us into a wealthy place."* Again, it takes courage to reach your wealthy place or Higher Ground.

Now, let's examine Joshua and his journey to the Promised Land. In Joshua 1:9 (NKJV), God instructs Joshua to, *"Be strong and of a good courage; be not afraid, neither be thou dismayed; for the Lord thy God is with thee whithersoever thou goest."* Focus on the word "dismayed" for a moment. To be dismayed means to feel distressed, worried and confused usually because one is experiencing a difficult situation. From these Biblical passages we can also derive the definition for courage, which is the product of my determination to complete God's task regardless of the circumstances. Courage means to possess and put forth the boldness and bravery required to succeed. To pursue wealth God's way you must have courage.

God also tells Joshua, *"For then thou shalt make thy way prosperous and then thou shalt have good success"* (Joshua 1:8, *NKJV).* Since God told Joshua that he could have good success, obviously there is another kind of success to reach God's goal. However, as believers we know that God's way is extremely different from man. The Scripture declares that "there us is a way that seemeth right to man but the end thereof is death." As you can see, God has a way that He wants to bring us to Higher Ground. He wants everyone to have a personal journey where the experience is such that only God can be credited for taking you to Higher Ground.

In Deuteronomy 8, God spoke to the children of Israel through Moses' message of financial prosperity. God called the children of Israel to Higher Ground. They had just spent more than 400 years in slavery and were finally coming out 40 years in the wilderness with Moses. This prophet delivered a God-inspired message of prosperity, where God promises to, "Bringeth thee into a good land" (Deuteronomy 8:7, NKJV).

However, there is a price to pay for eternal abundance. God wants you to courageously honor Him and the covenant set forth. Deuteronomy 8:17-18 (NKJV) states, *"And thou say in thine heart, my power and the might of mine hand hath gotten me this wealth. But thou shalt remember the Lord thy God, for it is he that giveth the power to get wealth, that he may establish his covenant which he swore unto thy fathers, as it is this day."* Clearly, God wants you to know with certainty that it was He who brought you to Higher Ground. People always want to give someone else the credit. But, it is God who brought us this far. And if God doesn't help us, we can't get any help.

God has a way of bringing you up to Higher Ground - a place of abundance and financial wealth. It is indeed a place of safety. To get there, we cannot serve both man's way and God's way. God's plan for increase is that you become a happy, willing and cheerful giver. Man's way is "a bird in the hand is better than two in the bush." Man's way says, "Since I already have something, why give it away?" You must choose to focus on God's method of attaining prosperity.

When you are going to Higher Ground you have to give more. You can only have one master. Luke 6:38 (NKJV) states, *"Give, and it shall be given unto you good measure, pressed down and shaken together, and running over, shall men give unto your bosom. For with the same measure that ye mete withal it shall be measured to you again."* Some of you are passing prosperity and abundance and reaching higher ground by your own way. You took your rebellious chances because you don't really believe that God can bless you if you did it His way. Many of you work all the overtime you can and do all the side jobs (or hustles) while your spiritual life suffers. Leaders cannot afford to do this.

Matthew 6:22 (NKJV) reminds us: The light of the body is the eye: if therefore thine eye be single they whole body shall be full of light." This Scripture demonstrates that wherever your focus is placed, there too, you will receive deeper revelation. My focus determines what masters my life. Now examine what this Scripture goes on to say: *"But if thine eye be evil, thy whole body shall be full of darkness. If therefore the light that* is *in thee be darkness, how great* is *that darkness! No man can serve two masters: for either he will hate the one, and love the other: or else he will hold to the one, and despise the other. You cannot serve God and mammon" (Matthew* 6:23-24, *NKJV).*

You cannot serve both God and the world's system. You cannot serve both God and money. You will have to place money, financial prosperity and financial wealth in their proper perspective. Most people love money even though they don't have any. Your financial state in life will be a product of what you think about money. Think about it.

Money does not go to places where it is needed nor does it go to places where it is desired. If money did either of these two things, many people who don't have money would have it. Money is attracted to those who understand and respect its seed potential. If that seed is placed in the proper ground, then it will create a harvest. When seed is linked with the proper soil, it will break through concrete. When you know how to link your seed with covenant soil, it will create a power that will break any barrier that attempts to keep you from prospering God's way—which is the best method.

God's way is giving—yet giving money is a grievous thought to some people. Many people like to make fun of the rich ruler in the Bible who Jesus confronted. But I do not think many of us can question the ruler's thoughts. In Mark 10:17-22 (NKJV), the Bible shows how the concept of money rules the minds of many. *"Then Jesus beholding him loved him, and said unto him, one thing thou lackest: go thy way, sell whatsoever thou hast, and give to the poor, and thou shalt have treasure in heaven: and come, take up the cross, and follow me. And he was sad at that saying, and went away grieved: for he had great possessions."* The rich young ruler made a decision about the offering that Jesus asked of him before he understood the message. Most people have the same attitude about money as the rich young ruler. It is grievous for most people to give to the church.

They do not see the joy and gain in giving because the world's system has corrupted their minds so much that they are deceived and misguided. The world's philosophy says, "Get all you can." However, God's way is totally different from the world's self-centered theories. You must begin to shift your focus from getting all you can to becoming a distribution channel of supply. I am a receiver so now can sow. The Scripture states, "He giveth deed to the sower," (Isaiah 55: 10, NKJV). The sower is the person who lives to give. When you talk about prosperity and finances, it first touches the flesh because the flesh is greedy. You must admit that when you first think about prosperity and money, you are not thinking about giving a dime to anybody.

You are thinking, "It's now that I can get this and that." You know there is a move of God and you are saying, "Maybe this is my lucky day." There has to be some corrections made in your thought process if you are going to get blessed God's way. You have to see yourself living to give, and then you will always have enough because God will always give you seed. He gives seed to the sower, bread for you to eat and He will multiply the seed sown. "As it is written, He hath dispersed abroad; he hath given you the poor; his righteousness remaineth forever. Now he that ministereth seed to the sower both ministers bread for your food, and multiply your seed sown, and increase the fruits of your righteousness," (2 Corinthians 9:9-10, NKJV).

God wants to use you to cause others to give thanks and glory to Him. You have to get selfishness out of your thinking. God's way is for you to stop saying, "I am going to get all I can for me." You can reach Higher Ground. You can obtain material possessions for yourself- but sowing must be your priority. You should desire to be a channel through which God can bless others. This is the adjustment you will have to make. You have to get out of the rat race. This is no longer a "dog-eat-dog" situation.

Leaders are no longer backstabbers and do anything to get to the top. That's not God's way. Your mindset has to be, "I want God to make me a blessing in the Earth." God instructed Abraham about reaching his wealthy place or Higher Ground. One of the provisions was that He would make Abram a blessing. God said to Abram, "I want to bless you so you can be a blessing to others." That is the key to getting it God's way. Sowing takes courage. It requires you to be bold enough to step out into new territory. As leaders we have to declare that God is our source and that we should never look in any other direction.

"Now the Lord had said unto Abram, Get out of thy country, and from thy kindred, and from thy father's house, unto a land that I will show thee. And I will make of thee a great nation, and I will bless thee, and make thy name great, and thou shall be a blessing" (Genesis 12:1, NKJV). That is the key, "thou shall be a blessing." God has placed the desire to be a blessing to others in your heart. The devil has corrupted that desire and caused you to become selfish in life. How many times have we, as children growing up, witnessed our parents struggling and desired to get to a place of blessing so that we could be a blessing to them?

How many of you have seen needs in the Earth and were stirred with a desire to do something about it? The desire to move to Higher Ground has always been in our heart. But, over the course of time, the god of mammon crushed your dreams. We became very selfish with thoughts of, "all for me, mine and no more." The attitude of the people is that they have obtained what they possess by themselves and nobody helped them. So, why should they help someone else? You should help others because that is God's way. You must begin to see yourself as a blessing in the Earth. The promise of wealth to move to Higher Ground for the believer is clearly revealed in the Bible. The Bible says a poor man's words are not heard.

But, God wants us to be heard!

Proverbs 10:22 (NKJV) states, "The blessing of the Lord, it maketh rich, and he addeth no sorrow with it." Rich is plain old rich. God said we are on our way to Higher Ground (our wealthy place) because God wants to increase us more and more so we can do more and more to His glory. Psalm 115:12 (NKJV) offers an incredible promise from God. "*He will bless them that fear the Lord, both small and great. The Lord shall increase you more and more, you and your children.*"

The phrase "more and more" in this Scripture is the reason why we should define the wealthy place as a continuous effort and process of increase. No matter how well things are for you now, there is a higher place for you. There is a financial abundance that is promised in the word of God. It is also that which is necessary for you to fulfill your purpose of being a blessing in the Earth. God wants you to go to Higher Ground: He wants to show you off to everybody else. The Scripture says that the eyes of the Lord run to and fro throughout the whole Earth in search of someone to show off. Leaders, maintain your courage and you'll make it to Higher Ground!

CHALLENGE

Write down a list of five issues and situations that you are afraid of in leadership? Areas where you know your courage is waning. This is probably an area where you do not want to deal with because of some conflict.

Write down your limitations. It will take courage to address them. So write down one step you will take to conquer your limitations.

Courage is the ability to be bold (The devil will talk you against it and make you feel bad for not "deserving" this). Be confident that this is where God wants you to be and it is part of the plan of God and if you don't have the boldness you will never come here. I remember when a husband wanted his wife to try on very expensive shoes, and she would say, "No, I'm not going to spend this kind of money". She liked the shoes. The husband wanted her to have boldness and courage to wear the shoes. Finally, she tried them only to realize she could wear them. The next weekend someone blessed her with the same shoes for Mother's Day. You have to have the boldness to walk in the prosperity that God has planned for you.

Leadership is lonely you are out front you have to make decisions by yourself. You still have to operate in the area you are called to, relying on God to give you the strength to stand.

Key #15: Stand Loyal

There is a difference between faithfulness and loyalty. Faithfulness is an action. A person who is faithful demonstrates an action but does not tell us anything about his heart or motives. On the other hand, loyalty describes a person's heart—his attitude. In fact, loyalty is a term that describes a positive attitude that honors the one being served. A loyal person operates without a self-seeking motive to serve. Loyalty is the part of love that seeketh not her own. Globally (church, home, workplace and family), there is a great need for trust! A ministry's effectiveness is limited to how much you can trust one another. The moment we mistrust someone, our ability to receive from him is reduced. If your trust grows, your capacity to receive grows.

For example, if someone comes up with a prophetic word, your ability to receive him or her is directly tied to how much you trust that person. In I Thessalonians 5:12, the Apostle Paul writes, *"Know them that labor among you."* That's more than a handshake. The Kingdom of God is built on trust not love. I am commanded to love you. I'm not commanded to trust you. When a wife has a husband who has been unfaithful, she is commanded to forgive, but not trust. She is not even commanded to stay married. Sure, you can have gifts, abilities and talents. But, they are not going to work, if trust is not present. Your gifts are not going to fulfill any ongoing purpose of God. You have to build trust.

You cannot be a devil all week, and suddenly become a saint on Sunday, and then expect to be received.

When you undermine the authority that God sets in place, you destroy your own home (2 Samuel 13:28-29). This pretentious behavior represents a spirit that can be in a man or woman.

God hates disloyalty. He builds on trust in a covenant family community. Marriages, families and churches are built on trust—not on spies and hidden cameras. Covenant, at its root, is trust not love. I can love you and not trust you. Love is unconditional (agape), but trust must be earned. You must build it and work to maintain the trust level. We are plagued with covenant breakers such as bankruptcy and divorces.

You must enter into covenant with God without any hidden motives or secret agendas.

Spiritually-developed gifts are given praise and reward character. And loyalty is an important character trait that God desires to see manifested correctly. Emphasis can be placed on the life of Absalom to give you a distinct perspective on how not to act as a future leader. For far too long, many congregations have been plagued by devious spirits, like Absalom, who claim to be "loyal" to God. Those spirits fell to the enemy's temptations and became evil spirits that desire self-gratification and self-promotion. To be an effective leader whose principal job is to promote the Gospel of Jesus Christ, you must always remember who you are and where your loyalty resides: within the Kingdom of God unselfishly.

CHALLENGE

The following are warning signs that you may have encountered an Absalom spirit:

1. Your spirit is independent and disloyal. (Proverbs 18:1).
1. You desire the praises of men. An Absalom spirit says, "Oh! If I were king."
2. You desire to continuously have your name read aloud or be upfront on the podium.

3. You seek the praise of men, which produces spiritual pride. You find yourself constantly asking, "Why doesn't everyone see it my way?"
5. You are personally wounded by any rejection of your ideas (2 Samuel 14:25-26).

Honestly look within yourself where you may possess any of these traits of Absalom and aggressively purge yourself of them all through consecration, prayer, and fasting. To move forward in leadership bearing an Absalom spirit is an abomination to the call on your life and will bring forth a curse on the ministry you are currently under and the ministry you could eventually build once this spirit is stripped.

www.ingramcontent.com/pod-product-compliance
Lightning Source LLC
Chambersburg PA
CBHW050645160426
43194CB00010B/1819